Canada's
BASTIONS
of EMPIRE

Canada's BASTIONS of EMPIRE

Halifax, Victoria and the Royal Navy 1749–1918

Bryan Elson

Formac Publishing Company Limited
Halifax

Notice to educators
This book is available for purchase in print and ebook form. Copies can be purchased from our website at www.formac.ca. Copies of individual chapters or portions of the full text in print or digital form are also available for sale at reasonable prices. Contact us for details at rights@formac.ca.

The publisher and the author of this work expect that portions of this work will be useful for education, and expect reasonable compensation for this use. This can be readily achieved by arranging to purchase these portions from the publisher. Contrary to the view of university administrators and their legal advisors, it is unlikely that use of a chapter or 10% of this work for educational purposes with no payment to the publisher or author would be found to be fair dealing under the Canadian Copyright Act.

Formac Publishing Company Limited recognizes the support of the Province of Nova Scotia through the Department of Communities, Culture and Heritage. We are pleased to work in partnership with the province to develop and promote our culture resources for all Nova Scotians. We acknowledge the financial support of the Government of Canada through the Canada Book Fund for our publishing activities. We acknowledge the support of the Canada Council for the Arts for our publishing program.

Cover design: Tyler Cleroux

Library and Archives Canada Cataloguing in Publication

Elson, Bryan, author
    Canada's bastions of empire / Bryan Elson.

Includes bibliographical references and index.
Issued in print and electronic formats.
ISBN 978-1-4595-0326-7 (bound).--ISBN 978-1-4595-0327-4 (epub)

    1. Canada--History, Naval. 2. Canada. Royal Canadian Navy--
History--World War, 1914-1918. 3. World War, 1914-1918--Naval
operations, Canadian. 4. Navy-yards and naval stations--Canada--
History. I. Title.

FC231.E47 2014   359.00971   C2014-903101-7
                                       C2014-903102-5

Formac Publishing Company Limited
5502 Atlantic Street
Halifax, Nova Scotia, Canada
B3H 1G4
www.formac.ca

Printed and bound in Canada

CONTENTS

*As always, for Maxine and Christopher, and for my father
Edgar John Elson, twice wounded in the Great War.*

INTRODUCTION

The voluminous literature on Canada's participation in the Great War of 1914–1918 contains very little information on its home defences; only six pages of 596 in Volume 1 of the official history. For the army, the glorious story of the Canadian Expeditionary Force in France completely overshadows the unglamorous work of the thousands of men who manned the eastern and western coastal fortresses continually from the first day of the war to the last. Relatively better documented is the work of the infant Royal Canadian Navy. Unfortunately it too was condemned to a humdrum role, thanks to earlier governmental neglect. With no opportunity for heroes to shine forth it produced none. Not for these forgotten soldiers and sailors the stirring deeds of their overseas compatriots; simply four years of unremitting strain and later exclusion from the national memory.

The dearth of historical information is paralleled by a striking lack of personal accounts. The stressful but largely routine nature of home service did not lend it itself to the writing of memoirs such as those that emerged from the years of trench warfare. For men serving very largely in their own communities the need to write letters home was much less pressing, and those that were written would contain little worth preserving about their monotonous routine. Nor would they have much of interest to transmit orally to succeeding generations of their families.

On June 28, 1914, in the Bosnian city of Sarajevo, a Serbian patriot named Gavrilo Princip assassinated the Archduke Franz Ferdinand, heir to the Austro-Hungarian thrones. Such was the bad blood between the two countries that war between them was a real possibility. In previous decades the major European powers had formed two rival alliances that could easily be drawn into a much wider war.

Canadians were aware that if Britain became a combatant it would mean that Canada would automatically be committed. But Europe was far away, and Canada itself seemed secure, facing no credible threat, and in any case was under the protection of the Royal Navy. That thousands of Canadian soldiers would eventually fight and die in the trenches of France was simply unimaginable.

But for two Canadian cities the perspective was very different. Halifax and Victoria were each home to a strategically important naval base, and for many years had been fortified and garrisoned for the purpose of defending them. Each was a provincial capital, a fact that in the case of Esquimalt was to become very important. They were 6,060 kilometres apart, with very different climates, economies and histories, but they shared the distinction of being the nation's coastal sentries, each a fortified stronghold protecting a naval base. In August 1914 that became an important reality differentiating them from all other Canadian cities.

This is the story of their response to threats, both actual and imaginary, as the possibility of war became real. Before turning to the critical events of 1914 the development of both places, as cities and as fortified naval bases, must be traced. In the nineteenth century, that development took place in an evolving political and strategic context, complicated by rapid changes in technology, and especially in military technology. By 1914, this complex and sometimes chaotic process had determined the capacities of the two bastions and the naval forces they protected to meet the challenges of war. As I researched the subject it became apparent that those capacities had been predetermined by the story of Canada itself in the 165 years between 1749 and 1914.

Underlying the entire story was one fundamental geopolitical constant. After the American Revolution, mainland British North America was made up of the scattered colonies of Nova Scotia, Prince Edward Island, and Lower and Upper Canada, each a separate entity with limited but growing self-government. The Hudson's Bay Company, chartered by Great Britain, traded in the vast expanse west of Hudson's Bay, as far as the Pacific, with no interference or political supervision from the homeland.

Throughout the period Canada was a dependency of Great Britain and part of the British Empire. Until 1867 the separate colonies were loosely grouped under the term British North America. Confederation united them in the Dominion of Canada, signifying that the new country was internally self-governing. However, Dominion status did not include control over foreign affairs or defence.

The mother country had full responsibility for the protection of this mostly wilderness part of the Empire. As a world power Britain's potential enemies were numerous. Her interests could and did conflict with those of European nations such as France and Russia, as evidenced by the Crimean War. But in the North American context only the United States really mattered. Whatever the cause of a war between the two, the obvious American strategy would be to invade Canada. That threat had a long history. During the Revolutionary War the Americans had unsuccessfully laid siege to Quebec, and a plan to attack Halifax was abandoned only when George Washington's spies learned that the place was more heavily defended than expected. During the War of 1812 several invasions took place at various points on the Great Lakes–St. Lawrence border.

It followed that British foreign and defence policy would determine the security of British North America and, later, Canada. The views of the various colonies and the later Dominion were very much secondary to the broader interests of the empire as a whole, as conceived by the British government. Sometimes they coincided; if not, it would often be imperial rather than colonial interests that took precedence. For Canada's coastal fortresses imperial interests were synonymous with the strategic interests of the Royal Navy: those defences were there to protect the naval bases from which the strongest navy in the world would sally forth to implement imperial policy. They provided the Navy with the land bases required in the event that Britain would find itself in conflict with the United States, and with a need to project its naval power along the American coast to strangle trade and to put pressure on the United States government. Or to mount an attack, as happened in the War of 1812. They also gave the British government the military presence necessary for an authoritative response to any attempt by the United States to invade or annex Canada — an idea that, as we will see, was openly discussed at various times in the nineteenth century as the new country expanded its territory in every direction but north.

After Canada's 1867 emergence as an internally self-governing dominion Britain retained control of its foreign affairs and defence. But as nascent Canadian nationalism became stronger the country began its journey from colony to nation. That journey would be complicated by the ambiguity of entrusting the defence of a would-be nation to the armed forces of the mother country. These tensions were played out and reflected in the development of the coastal fortresses and of the Canadian navy.

As emerging powers gathered strength in the late nineteenth century Great Britain's international position gradually weakened in relative terms. Until the First World War the basic obligation to defend her colonies was never formally abandoned; but her willingness and ability to do so was gradually eroded.

And there was a second underlying geopolitical constant: the influence of military technology on the development of the coastal strongholds. Although it had been static for a time, that technology began an extremely rapid period of change in the last quarter of the nineteenth century.

***

We are concerned here with Victoria and Halifax. The Pacific coast naval base and its defences have mainly been located in and around the former village and now municipality of Esquimalt, an integral part of the modern Victoria metropolitan area, but four miles to the west of the city centre. Henceforth, "Esquimalt" will indicate the location of military developments related to the naval base; "Victoria" will refer to the entire urban area. On the Atlantic coast, the base and it defences are all within the city proper, and "Halifax" accurately covers both.

The Oxford Dictionary defines *fortress* as "a military stronghold, especially a strongly fortified town fit for a large garrison." That definition most definitely applies to Halifax. Along with Malta, Gibraltar, and Bermuda, it was one of the four great fortresses of the overseas British Empire. In comparison with other places on the Pacific coast, Esquimalt was indeed a military stronghold, but its strategic importance was always considerably less than that of Halifax, as was its material strength. With that limitation understood, in what follows the term "fortress" will apply to both places, as will the principles governing their construction and armament.

A fortress could be threatened either by sea or by land; the defences therefore needed to be able to repel attacks from both directions. Their armament had to be capable of successfully engaging attacking forces that were equipped with the latest weaponry. The location of the defending batteries might no longer be appropriate to the nature and scale of new forms of attack, and the fortresses' guns needed to be upgraded as rapidly as those of the potential attackers.

It will be important also to understand the changing roles of the human defenders, the "garrison," of the fortresses. For most of the period the permanent garrisons at both places were British, until the British were withdrawn under the pressure of events. The permanent garrisons were never strong enough in themselves to provide an effective defence. In emergency, the Canadian militia would have to be mobilized in support.

Until late in the period Canada did not possess either a navy or a regular army. However, since the days of the French regime it had always had a militia, consisting, in theory, of all fit males. In an emergency they were subject to be called up and paid for the duration of their service. In peacetime a small proportion of volunteers were designated "active militia" and were paid while undergoing part-time training. When there was no threat on the horizon resources were always stinted, and the active militia would decline in numbers and effectiveness until rejuvenated by the next crisis. Apart from the active volunteers, at any given time the great body of the militia was quite untrained and of no military value.

CHAPTER ONE
The Watch Is Set,
1749–1858

It was British foreign and defence policy that determined the security of British North America. As a world power Britain had numerous potential enemies, but her policy was one of splendid isolation. Up until the early twentieth century she refrained from entering into permanent alliance with any other power, relying on her enormously powerful navy and the fortresses and bases that sheltered and supported it. These coastal bastions in Canada and elsewhere around the world were designed and built to resist all comers, but at any given time the immediate threat would emanate from a particular rival.

When war broke out in 1914, Britain had made Canada part of its strategic thinking for more than 150 years, and a long-established military presence in the colonies that ultimately became Canada.

***

1776 defences of Halifax, third reconstruction.

Halifax had a military purpose from its very beginning, the enemy of the time being France. On June 21, 1749, Governor Edward Cornwallis landed at Chedabucto with about 2500 settlers carried in 15 vessels. There were a number of possible sites for a new town on both sides of the harbour, but Cornwallis chose what has since become the present city's downtown waterfront area and christened the town Halifax after Lord Halifax, president of the British Board of Trade.

The navy was satisfied as the site offered safe anchorage in deep water but close to shore. There were three hundred miles of roadless wilderness between Halifax and Louisbourg, the French fortress on Cape Breton Island, and the only way a strong force of regular troops could move between them was by sea. As long as a superior squadron was available the Royal Navy could be counted upon to intercept and thwart any such attempt by the French. But, just in case, three artillery batteries were also established on the shoreline, pointing to seaward.

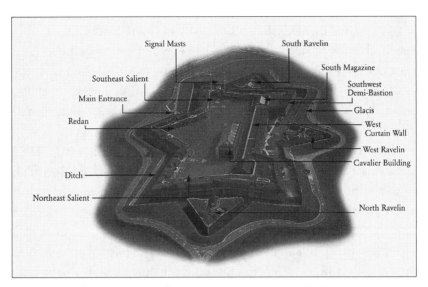

The layout of Halifax Citadel after reconstruction in the mid-1800s. It soon became obsolete as weapon technology made rapid improvements.

Cornwallis was more concerned with the defensibility of the place from land attack by Quebec rangers and their native and Acadian allies. Capable of rapid and secretive movement, they were formidable opponents in irregular frontier warfare. Accordingly, he constructed a rough half-circle of wooden palisades running down to the shore to enclose the town, strengthened at intervals by wooden blockhouses. These would not have withstood a siege by French regulars for more than a few days, but were invulnerable to assault by an enemy devoid of artillery or experience in siege warfare. In the first few years numerous settlers were killed outside the fixed defences, but none within the makeshift wooden walls.

Initially, the Royal Navy's interest in Halifax was limited to securing an anchorage from which to launch an attack on Louisbourg and then Quebec. It was soon recognized, though, that the harbour could also be developed to provide maintenance and supply services. In 1759 the King's Yard was established on the shore immediately north of the town, and Cornwallis's original defences were improved by several new forts whose guns commanded the entrance channel. During the American Revolution George Washington saw Halifax as a critical British strategic asset, but was deterred from attacking it when spies determined that it was much better defended than had been thought.

The symbiosis between a naval base and its army land defences had emerged. The scale of such defences was critical, and in this respect the navy ultimately had the deciding word. If the Royal Navy identified a strategically significant base, the army would eventually have to construct and man a fortress sufficiently strong to satisfy the sailors. Thus the navy would be free to pursue its blue-water tasks, confident that its vital shore support would continue to be available when needed. Conversely, the navy would not show much interest in the land defences of a port to which it attached little strategic importance. The contrasting developments of Esquimalt and Halifax would reflect this reality as it played out in the Canadian context.

Except for one brief interval, the British garrisoned Halifax from its 1749 founding until 1906. In addition to artillery and engineers, two infantry battalions were normally in residence; nearly three thousand British troops in all on Nova Scotian and later Canadian soil. It would be difficult to exaggerate the importance of this military presence. It made a critical contribution to the economic base of the community, particularly when large-scale fortress construction was under way. Socially, the presence of large numbers of upper-class British officers gave the place an atmosphere of sophistication and gaiety far exceeding the typical colonial outpost, particularly during the governorship of Prince Edward, one of the sons of George III, at the end of the eighteenth century.

Accompanied by his mistress, Prince Edward very much enjoyed himself, while taking a real interest in the defences.

Notably, he established a visual telegraph system between the outer forts and central Fort George, and eventually as far as Windsor. Arms mounted on a line of towers could be manipulated to spell out messages, repeated from one station to the next until they reached the addressee. By this means he was able to micromanage his troops from his retreat on the shore of Bedford Basin, much to the chagrin of his officers.

The key to the defence of Halifax was a 225-foot rise to the west of the town, now known as Citadel Hill, on which Cornwallis had originally erected the wooden blockhouse, Fort George. It was replaced or improved upon in 1761, 1777, and again in 1793, at times when war was threatened or actually occurring. Between these flurries of activity the fortifications were allowed to deteriorate. In 1825 an investigation led to a decision to completely redevelop the old fort according to the latest principles and using the strongest of materials. The new work would be the main defence against enemy troops assumed to have been landed at St. Margaret's Bay or Lawrencetown, or approaching overland from the Bay of Fundy or New Brunswick. In addition, it would mount cannons pointing to seaward to help counter a seaborne attack.

Construction began in 1828. The desired footprint involved the removal of the relics of previous works and lowering the height of the hill by twenty feet. Slowed by the climate, poor workmanship, and faulty design, construction was not completed until 1858. At that time Halifax was recognized as one of the most powerful fortresses in the British Empire, and a strong bastion against the demonstrated threat of American expansionism northwards.

Except in wartime the naval presence was more sporadic. During the War of 1812 Halifax was the base from which the British acquired sea control along the Atlantic coast, eventually driving the United States Navy and merchant marine from the high seas. At such times Water Street swarmed with sailors, often engaging in fierce street fights with each other or with soldiers from the barracks around the citadel; at that time Brunswick Street was in fact called Barrack Street. Prostitution and drunkenness were endemic; it was said that "the business of half the town was to sell rum, and the business of the other half to drink it." Respectable citizens were careful to avoid the streets at night.

The Royal Naval operating area in the western Atlantic was known as the North America and West Indies Station. In 1819 its headquarters and the principal support functions were concentrated at Bermuda, an important development which left the Halifax dockyard in caretaker status. However, each summer the squadron visited Halifax for an extended period, and the commanding admiral occupied the official residence, which still stands and houses an excellent museum. This operational cycle conveniently allowed the squadron to avoid both the Caribbean hurricane season and the Canadian winter.

The two Treaties of Paris in 1763 and 1783 ended the Seven Years' War and the American War of Independence, respectively. Once a major North American power, France had lost all its mainland territories. But beginning in the early nineteenth century a new threat to British North America was gradually coming into view.

Spain, a declining power, ruled Mexico, including Texas, New Mexico, and California. It also possessed the former French territory of Louisiana, nearly 900,000 square miles comprising the basin of the Missouri–Mississippi river system. On paper Mexico and everything west of the Mississippi River was recognized as Spanish territory, as were East and West Florida.

Russian fur traders had begun crossing the Bering Strait to Alaska in the 1740s, and by 1783 there was some settlement, and its claim had been defined and mapped, not always accurately.

Britain retained her colonies of Quebec, Nova Scotia, and New Brunswick, and Loyalists fleeing the Revolution began to occupy the area that would in 1791 become Upper Canada, now Ontario. Since 1690 the Hudson's Bay Company had held trading rights within the watersheds of all the rivers flowing into Hudson's Bay, as far west as the continental divide. This tract of more than one and a half million square miles contained a few settlements and trading posts.

The newly independent United States had expanded from its seaboard confines into the formerly French possessions east of the Mississippi. With alacrity the colonists occupied the land. Where the natives resisted they were defeated with great loss, and forced into treaty relationships or deported west of the Mississippi.

The United States had almost by accident possessed itself of Spain's territory of Louisiana. It had been French until ceded to Spain in 1762, but was secretly transferred back. In 1800 Napoleon Bonaparte conceived a plan to re-establish a French presence in North America, but was forced to abandon it when war again broke out between Britain and France. Needing funds for the invasion of England, Napoleon sold Louisiana to the United States for twenty-five million dollars. The Louisiana Purchase conveyed the Missouri–Mississippi watershed to the United States, at an average cost of four cents per square mile.

This enormous tract would in time encompass all or part of twelve future American states. Two small rivers in what are now Alberta and Saskatchewan flowed to the Missouri–Mississippi system; thus their watersheds would theoretically become American. On the other hand the Red River valley drained to Hudson Bay and thus belonged to the Hudson Bay Company's Rupert's Land.

After the Revolution most of the boundary between the United States and British North America ran along the centre line of the St. Lawrence–Great Lakes waterway. With the Louisiana Purchase it was necessary to extend the line across the

Purchased from France in 1803, Louisiana at that time encompassed the entire Mississippi–Missouri watershed west of the Mississippi. The vast area would later include many American states and bring American territory to the Canadian border west of the Great Lakes.

prairies. Under the Jay Treaty of 1818 the extension was surveyed from the northwest angle of Lake of the Woods, in latitude 49 degrees north, without deviation as far as the continental divide. As a result the small areas in the Missouri watershed remained British, but much of the watershed of the Red River which led to Fort Garry was lost, and eventually became part of North Dakota rather than Manitoba.

No British colonists were involved in these negotiations, probably very few were even aware of them, but a pattern that would later become important had been established. The interests of native Americans — in particular, of the First Nations warriors who fought on the British side in the War of 1812 — received little consideration.

***

By treaty or purchase, America expanded beyond the Mississippi into the northwestern watershed of the great river. But vast areas of the continent still beckoned, unsettled, undeveloped, and loosely held by Spain/Mexico, Russia, and Great Britain. Nineteenth-century American politicians — and large segments of the American public — saw continued expansion of the United States into these territories as natural, desirable — in fact for many it was God's will. These views were captured in the doctrine of Manifest Destiny which held that these territories really belonged by right to the United States, which alone was capable of making them fruitful, as God had intended. This revelation justified the use of any means, including violence, to wrest the remainder of the continent from the hands of its unworthy possessors.

As articulated by John Louis O'Sullivan in relation to the Oregon Territory dispute, the United States should claim the whole region "by the right of our manifest destiny to overspread and to possess the entire continent." In *Sword of the Spirit, Shield of Faith*, American historian Andrew Preston identifies the pervasive influence of religion on American domestic and foreign policies from independence to the present day. He notes:

> *Manifest destiny exerted a strong pull on*
> *America's religious imagination, especially the*
> *notions that the United States was a blessed land,*
> *that its citizens were God's chosen people, and*
> *that America was providentially ordained to*
> *spread its blessings of liberty far and wide.*

Not all Americans shared these views, of course, but their neighbours were naturally wary and alarmed by the notion of divinely mandated expansion.

***

Spain was the first to be menaced. In 1810 President Madison proclaimed the annexation of West Florida, the Gulf coast panhandle. In 1817 an American offer to purchase peninsular East Florida was rejected by Spain, and the United Sates proceeded to occupy the territory. Spanish resistance was easily overcome, showing how weak its hold was on its North American possessions. In no position to resist, it accepted a cash payment to abandon its claims west of the continental divide and north of the 42nd parallel.

In this purchase the United States acquired a coastline on the Pacific Ocean, between what remained in Spanish hands south of latitude 42 degrees, and the disputed Oregon Territory to the north.

When in 1821 Mexico secured its independence, the remaining Spanish territory in North America passed to the new republic, which was only marginally more capable than Spain of defending it. In 1836 Mexico was forced to accept the establishment of an independent republic in its state of Texas. In 1845 United States President John Tyler signed a bill annexing Texas and granting it immediate American statehood. When Mexico did not react, American troops advanced beyond the Texas border to the Rio Grande. Provoked beyond endurance, Mexico declared war in 1846. After a two year struggle the Americans dictated peace in Mexico City. In addition to Texas, Mexico was stripped of its states of New Mexico and upper California, but was allowed to retain desolate Baja California.

As already mentioned, by the agreement of 1818 the 49th parallel boundary between the United States and British North America was extended only as far west as the continental divide. Between the divide and the west coast, what became known as the Oregon Territory was in dispute between Britain and the United States. It comprised the area north of 42 degrees north (the formerly Spanish, now American, California line), and south of the Russian Alaska boundary of 54 degrees 40 minutes north. In 1818 the two countries had agreed to joint occupation pending the resolution of a final boundary. Britain had granted the Hudson's Bay Company trading rights in the whole area, and it exercised its authority in the territory using the laws of Upper Canada.

Negotiations between Britain and the United States failed to produce a final agreement on how the Territory was to be divided. In the meantime, American settlers moved into the Willamette Valley south of the Columbia River, the classic first step in the process used elsewhere by the United States which led to annexation. There was no settlement by citizens of either country north of the Columbia and south of the 49th parallel, but the British claimed the area on the basis of long usage by the Hudson's Bay Company and the discoveries of its explorers.

The American claim was based on the extension of the 49th parallel to the coast and beyond to include that portion of Vancouver Island lying south of the 49th.

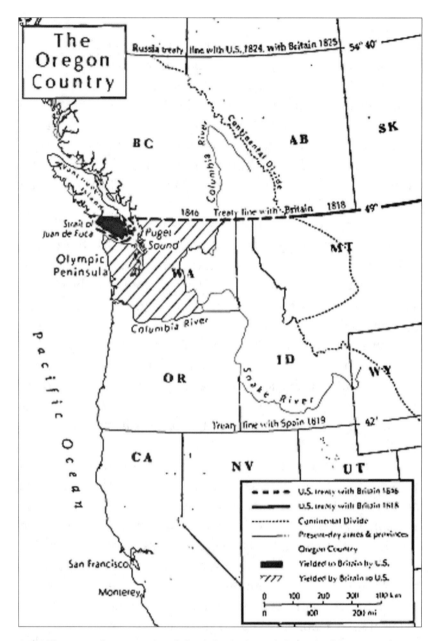

Map illustrates the competing claims of Britain and the United States on the west coast. The compromise agreement led to the establishment of the Hudson's Bay Company's Pacific headquarters at Victoria.

Founding of Victoria by James Douglas, later governor of British Columbia. This new Pacific headquarters of the Hudson's Bay Company was made necessary by the settlement of the Oregon Territory dispute.

The British position involved extending the 49th parallel line only until it reached the Columbia River, about halfway between the divide and the coast. From that point it would follow the lower reaches of that river south and west to the coast, at what is now Astoria, Washington. The Hudson's Bay fort, Fort Vancouver, on the north bank of the Columbia, in what is now the city of Vancouver, Washington, would be British territory.

In the presidential election of 1844 the Democratic candidate James K. Polk announced that as president he would cease negotiating, and acquire the whole of the Oregon Territory to the Russian Alaska boundary by force, cutting off British North America from access to the Pacific. Following the campaign the alliterative slogan "Fifty-Four Forty or Fight" was enthusiastically taken up by the militant expansionists.

While taking this aggressive stand Polk felt able to state:

> *The world has nothing to fear from military ambition in our Government. While the Chief Magistrate and the popular branch of Congress are elected for short terms by the suffrages of those millions who must in their own persons bear all the burdens and miseries of war, our Government can not be otherwise than pacific.*

Britain reacted to Polk's threat and his election in 1845 with ostentatious military preparations. The British government was nonetheless cautious; crop failures in the U.K. made imports of large quantities of American wheat important to Britons. As for the Americans, they were about to provoke a conflict with Mexico. They risked fighting two wars at the same time, and a possible Mexican–British alliance. The eastern states would suffer most from a potential British naval blockade, in pursuit of territorial gains from which they would derive little or no benefit. The south foresaw that new states emerging from the Oregon acquisition would tip the free-state/slave-state balance against them. National interests dictated that a way should be found to avoid Polk's promised annexation.

A settlement was formalized in the Oregon Treaty of June 1846. The line of the 49th parallel was extended to the coast, but no further. Thus, Britain retained the whole of Vancouver Island, but gave up the Hudson's Bay Company's grant between the Columbia and the 49th parallel. Fort Vancouver became a United States army base, preserved today with re-enactors playing its Hudson's Bay employees.

In signing the Oregon Treaty, the British government unilaterally disposed of lands that could and should have later become part of the new nation. British disregard of the interests of its loyal colonists was clear.

Extending the boundary along the 49th parallel created a problem for the Hudson's Bay Company, with its important coastal trading interests. Its western headquarters was in the area ceded to the United States, and a new location had to be found. At the time, the man directing the company's west-coast activities was James Douglas. Born in Scotland, he received a good education before joining the North West Company, a rival to the Hudson's Bay Company until the two firms merged. He served in steadily more responsible positions at company forts in Rupert's Land

and the Oregon Territory. At one of his early posts he married the daughter of his superior and his aboriginal wife. Unlike many other European fur traders, Douglas formalized his marriage at a Church of England ceremony some years later. Douglas remained devoted to his wife and large family throughout his life.

Since 1843 a minor trading post had existed on a narrow harbour at the southeast tip of Vancouver Island. Douglas decided to make it the new area headquarters. He enlarged the tiny existing fort (on the site of today's Bastion Square). French-Canadian employees of the company strengthened the wooden palisade with two bastions, using logs supplied by the Songhees band. Fort Victoria was never attacked or even threatened, and was demolished in 1864.

In his dealings with the native inhabitants Douglas was firm but fair. They never offered an organized threat to the post. Incidents that occurred were treated as criminal acts rather than warlike attacks. To arrest a suspected murderer from the Cowichan band Douglas organized a small unit of Victoria Voltigeurs from the company's servants, and carried them to the area in Her Majesty's Ship *Beaver*. A jury was empaneled and the accused was tried on the *Beaver*'s quarterdeck.

The British government established Vancouver Island as a partially self-governing Crown colony in 1849. Douglas was appointed governor in 1851, while retaining his position with the company. He began the development of the Nanaimo coalfields and protected them with a blockhouse, First Nations lands were purchased and reserves laid out, roads were built, and schools established. Farming, sawmilling, and salmon fishing enterprises began to thrive. He never wavered in his determination to resist American encroachments that might eventually lead to the absorption of the Vancouver Island colony and the mainland area north of the 49th parallel.

During his long service Douglas never took a furlough nor was absent even one day from duty. As colonial governor, he dedicated himself to responsibility and toil. He could never consent "to represent her Majesty in a shabby way." In 1861 Lady Jane Franklin, wife of the Arctic explorer, visited Victoria. Her niece and travelling companion Sophia Cracroft wrote:

> *All people speak with great admiration of the Governor's intellect — and a remarkable man he must be to be thus fit to govern a Colony. He has read enormously we are told & is in fact a self educated man, to a point very seldom attained. His manner is singular, and you see in it the traces of long residence in an unsettled country, where the white men are rare & the Indians many. There is a gravity, & a something besides, which some might & do mistake for pomposity, but which is the result of long service in the H.B. Co's service, under the above circumstances . . .*

The governor's wife they found to be a woman with a gentle, simple, and kindly manner.

> *Have I explained that her mother was an Indian woman & that she keeps very much (far too much) in the background, indeed it is only lately that she has been persuaded to see visitors, partly because she speaks English with some difficulty, the usual language being either the Indian, or Canadian French . . .*

To the west of Fort Victoria was the commodious and almost landlocked harbour of Esquimalt, its shores a forest wilderness frequented only by the aboriginal inhabitants. In 1845, for the first time, a vessel of the Royal Navy visited the anchorage, perhaps prompted by the Oregon Territory dispute. By agreement with the Chileans, the Royal Naval squadron in the eastern Pacific had been using Valparaiso as its base. During the Crimean War of 1853–1856 there were naval engagements around the Kamchatka Peninsula in Russian Siberia, and a naval hospital was established on Duntze Head in Esquimalt harbour to care for the wounded.

Thus Esquimalt began to emerge as a factor in British defence strategy vis à vis both the Americans and the Russians. One hundred and eighteen Royal Engineers arrived in 1858 to construct the facilities for a small naval depot. Thereafter the Royal Navy maintained a sizable presence, reaffirming British North American interests against potential interlopers.

As in Halifax, the naval presence made an important contribution to the local economy. The ordinary British sailors were very popular. If a fire broke out in Victoria they would cheerfully run the four miles from Esquimalt to assist in extinguishing it. If one of them was jailed for a minor offence, citizens insisted that he be allowed to work independently, rather than in the chain gang with the other prisoners.

With seeming inevitability the naval base generated its own need to be defended. In 1859 there occurred the so-called Pig War, a bloodless conflict between Britain and the United States. Despite the absurd name, the incident could easily have resulted in full-scale conflict. The Oregon Treaty had left unresolved the ownership of the San Juan Islands in the middle of the strait dividing Vancouver Island from Oregon. A bilateral commission failed to settle the issue, and in 1856 it was referred back to the respective governments.

Douglas established a sheep ranch on San Juan Island, the largest of the group. Meanwhile, a few Americans began to settle there. A pig belonging to a company employee was shot by an American for eating the latter's potatoes. Compensation was offered but refused. When company authorities tried to arrest the settler a small number of American troops arrived. Governor

Douglas strongly urged the commander of the five-ship British naval squadron, Rear-Admiral Robert L. Baynes, to eject the interlopers. Two hundred marines were landed, but Baynes refused to begin hostilities, and the Vancouver Island Assembly dissuaded Douglas from stronger action.

The American detachment was also under orders not to fire the first shot. After a tense standoff and much negotiation both countries agreed to joint occupation pending negotiations. Ultimately it was necessary to resort to arbitration by an international commission. For the next twelve years the two garrisons coexisted very amicably; it is said that the biggest threat to peace was the large amount of alcohol available.

The mainland north of the American border remained Company territory, governmental authority being completely absent. In 1858 gold was discovered on the lower Fraser River. Douglas warned the British government that "If the country be thrown open to indiscriminate immigration the interests of the Empire may suffer." Miners and others who had failed to make their fortunes in the California rush of 1849 hurried north in their thousands, the vast majority Americans. Still without instructions from London, Douglas acted with speed and firmness. He decreed that they could only enter British territory at Victoria, where they were required to obtain a licence and to give up their firearms. Ship after ship dumped crowds of prospectors on the Victoria waterfront.

Enterprising businessmen from San Francisco opened new outfitting establishments in the town. A tent city sprang up, amply provided with makeshift saloons. Drunkenness, prostitution, and petty crime were rife; it was said that "half the inhabitants were convicts, and the other half deserved to be." A serious riot broke out when police attempted to arrest a drunken and belligerent prospector. The survey vessel Her Majesty's Ship *Plumper* was dispatched from the navy yard to Victoria harbour, and the landing of armed bluejackets quickly brought the disturbance to an end without further violence. Tensions in the town were somewhat abated when church groups arranged for two shiploads of marriageable young ladies to be brought into what had been a virtually all-male society.

The mainland remained a political vacuum with a continuing risk of chaos or even a takeover as the mainly American prospectors poured in. Douglas therefore moved swiftly to persuade the home government to create the mainland colony of British Columbia, with its capital at New Westminster. While retaining his same position on the Island, Douglas also became British Columbia's first governor in 1858. Over the objections of many mainlanders the two colonies were united in 1866 under the name British Columbia, the joint capital remaining in Victoria. Douglas had retired in 1864 amid the plaudits of the population. One of his previous detractors admitted, "I doubt if we shall ever have a better chief."

***

In 1838 a dispute had arisen over the boundary between Maine and New Brunswick. It was supposed to have been settled by the Jay Treaty of 1794, but the situation was very unclear due to conflicting maps and vague terminology. The area in question was centered on the Aroostook River, along which lumbermen from both Maine and New Brunswick had been felling timber for some time. When a New Brunswick sheriff arrested and jailed an American malefactor the Maine and Massachusetts militias were mobilized, and New Brunswick immediately followed suit. Later, regular troops from both the United States and the British garrison in Canada were also deployed, but no shots were fired. Apart from some brawls involving lumbermen the so-called Aroostook War was bloodless.

The New Brunswickers were mainly concerned with their right to exploit the valuable forests. The main focus of the British was to preserve the all-weather overland route from the Atlantic colonies to Quebec City, a vital connection that would have been in serious jeopardy if the full American claim had been allowed.

A British offer of arbitration was refused. Daniel Webster of the United States and Britain's Lord Ashburton negotiated a solution formalized in the Webster–Ashburton Treaty of 1842. The United States was awarded the larger portion of the disputed area, but the integrity of the British intercolonial route was preserved.

After the Treaty was concluded Webster produced a discredited map that had not figured in the negotiations. It appeared to show that the Americans had gained virtually all the territory under dispute, thus helping to ensure public acceptance in the United States. Lord Ashburton came under severe criticism. Experts on the subject later wrote:

> Unjust as such accusations are, it is nevertheless
> a fact that many Canadians still consider the
> Ashburton Treaty of 1842 to be the first and most
> important instance of the loss of Canadian rights
> due to the complacency of Great Britain and the
> crooked diplomacy of the United States.

The Crimean War in the early 1850s inaugurated a period of tension, caused by American diplomatic support of Russia, Britain's opponent. Again, war was a real possibility. In the great tradition of twisting the British lion's tail American newspapers and some politicians sided strongly with Russia. Although the American government maintained a strict neutrality the public clamour generated genuine fear north of the border. As we have seen, the Crimean War led to the establishment of the Esquimalt naval depot, and it had repercussions in Halifax, also. When the British garrison there departed for Crimea their role was, not very efficiently, assumed by the militia until the war was over.

***

By the 1860s both Victoria and Halifax had outlived their frontier days and were becoming well-developed communities. Halifax prospered mightily, based on one of the largest shipbuilding industries in the world. The Crimean War triggered a frenzy of new construction. The city's shipowners were active in trade with Europe, the Caribbean, and the United States. Railways were being built, connecting it with the rest of the province and into the Canadas, and numerous industries were established. Nevertheless, certain parts of the city retained their unsavoury reputation, as evidenced by a rough rhyme of the time:

> *I might a got a better suit if I'd a had the chance,*
> *I met a girl in Water Street, she asked me to a dance,*
> *I danced my own destruction, I'm stripped from head to feet;*
> *I stake my oath I'll go no more to a dance on Barrack Street.*
> *Come all you young sailor lads, a warning take by me,*
> *Be sure and choose your company when you go on a spree;*
> *Be sure keep out of Barrack Street or else you'll rue the day —*
> *With a woman's shirt and apron they'll rig you out for sea.*

The quiet village of Victoria was being transformed into a busy trading centre, in that respect a satellite of San Francisco. A newspaper was founded, Wells Fargo opened an office, and regular steamer service connected the growing town to the world.

CHAPTER TWO
Threat and Response,
1858–1905

The American Civil War of 1861–1865 was a watershed event, bringing into stark focus the geopolitical factors underlying the security of the scattered British colonies in North America. It was widely — and correctly — believed that Lincoln's secretary of state, William H. Seward, had a plan to annex Canada as a means of reconciling Confederates to the Union. When the Civil War began with the secession of the southern states an important objective of the rebel government was to obtain international recognition of the Confederacy as a separate nation. British public opinion generally opposed slavery and supported the Union cause. But the very important British clothing industry depended on supplies of cotton from the slave states, and on that basis the Confederates felt that the government could be influenced in their favour. Conversely, the Union was very suspicious of British intentions, even fearing that Britain might give military support to the Confederacy, hoping to reverse the result of the American Revolution.

Three serious controversies did erupt and contributed to a near-breakdown in British–American relationships.

Working through a British sympathizer a Confederate agent contracted for several armed commerce raiders to be built in British shipyards. The most effective was the Confederate States Ship *Alabama*, a single-screw steamer with auxiliary sails. In 1862 she sailed from the Liverpool yard with a civilian captain and crew, to rendezvous in the Azores with a supply ship carrying her Confederate officers and guns. With a crew attracted by high wages and the promise of prize money, she made numerous captures that seriously affected Union trade. She was eventually tracked down and sunk, but her exploits enraged the Union, who claimed that in allowing her to sail the British had committed a blatant breach of neutrality.

Meanwhile, the Confederate government appointed John Slidell and James Mason as emissaries to Britain to solicit support, up to and including military assistance. The Union was well aware of their mission, and the United States Navy was blockading the coast of the Confederacy. Slidell and Mason sailed from Charleston by night, eluding the blockade, and eventually arrived in Cuba. From there they embarked on the Royal Mail Ship *Trent*, which ran a scheduled service from the Caribbean.

At about noon on November 8, 1861, Captain Charles Wilkes of the USS *San Jacinto* forced the *Trent* to stop by firing shots across her bow. She was boarded, and Slidell, Mason, and their secretaries were taken aboard the *San Jacinto*, without resistance, but over the vehement protest of Captain James Moir of the *Trent*. Wilkes's justification was that the agents were contraband under the laws of the sea. If that were the case a prize crew should have been put aboard the *Trent* to steam her to a port with a prize court. This was not done.

Initially, the Union press and public were enthusiastic, as were President Lincoln and Secretary of State Seward. British press and public reaction was equally vigorous, but the British government had no wish to fight over the matter. Diplomatic efforts to find a face-saving exit for both sides were accelerated. It soon began to be realized that Wilkes's action was very similar to the Royal Navy's boarding of neutral American vessels during the Napoleonic wars to search for deserters and contraband, a practice that had contributed to the American decision to go to war in 1812. For the Americans, the prospect of war with the United Kingdom while simultaneously putting down a rebellion also had a sobering effect. The crisis ended when the Union released Mason and Slidell from their confinement at Boston.

A second incident caused renewed tension. Confederate sympathizers commandeered the American vessel *Chesapeake* off New England and sailed her to Saint John to take on coal. They then departed for Halifax with the intention of selling the cargo and arming the ship as a commerce raider. Pursued by the American Navy, they were overtaken in Nova Scotia territorial waters off Halifax and escorted into the port. The crew was found to include three Nova Scotians and a notorious Confederate privateer named George Wade. Before the matter could be adjudicated by the Halifax Court of Vice-Admiralty some prominent local citizens engineered Wade's escape by rowboat to the Dartmouth shore, where he vanished. Again the Americans were incensed, but tensions subsided when the court ruled that the *Chesapeake* should be returned to her American owners.

The British authorities realized that British forces in North America were totally inadequate to defend against a possible Union attack. In Nova Scotia there were just 2,100 regular troops, there were 2,200 in Upper and Lower Canada and New Brunswick, and a much smaller number at Esquimalt. Reinforcements were rushed to the colonies in chartered liners. By spring 1861 they totalled fourteen battalions of infantry, six batteries of field artillery and twelve of garrison artillery, plus engineers and service support. The St. Lawrence being frozen, a large contingent disembarked at Halifax and marched overland to Rivière du Loup, then on to Quebec and Kingston by rail.

Despite the reinforcements and the revitalization of the militia British strategy put the main emphasis on the navy. In the 1812–1814 war the Royal Navy had supported landing operations and placed major American ports under close blockade, ruining their trade and in the end bringing them to the negotiating table. Now the commander of the North Atlantic and West Indies Squadron, Rear-Admiral Sir Alexander Milne, was quickly reinforced. His ships were all steam propelled, while the Americans had many sailing vessels and converted merchant ships.

He had little doubt that he could secure control of the sea in any particular area, but how to use that control was a question. If there were to be another war with the United States the British had a plan to land 25,000 troops at New York and hold the place until the Americans sued for peace. But, concerned about civilian casualties, Milne was not prepared to bombard populated areas. He intended to use blockade in the event of any such conflict. Steam propulsion brought many advantages, but it meant that ships had to return to port quite frequently to replenish their coal stocks, whereas sailing navies had been able to remain on station for months on end. The value of Halifax in this scenario was evident. However, disruption of trade by blockade was not as easy as it had been. Nevertheless, it was the only strategy realistically available if war had actually broken out.

The colonies' own defence contribution consisted of their militias, in existence ever since the French regime in Quebec. In principle the militia was based on the concept of universal military service by all fit males between the ages of eighteen and sixty years. Attendance at annual musters was compulsory under penalty of a heavy fine. In an emergency, militiamen were drafted

York Redoubt, Halifax, 1860s. By this time it was becoming less important in the overall coastal defence plan.

by lot for a period not exceeding six months. If the emergency continued their places were taken by new drafts, but some units waived their rights and remained under arms for the duration. (A never-invoked last resort was the *levée en masse*, the compulsory call-up of the whole of the fit male population.) Such was the force that had fought the War of 1812, alongside the British regulars and Natives. The militia might supplement the British forces in emergencies, but in time of peace was entirely under the control of the different colonial governments.

Over the fifty years following the War of 1812–1814, the system had degenerated for lack of government support. No funds were allocated for paying, arming, or clothing the force, and many annual musters degenerated into alcoholic parties. There was no incentive for those interested in soldiering to make an effort to improve things. In Montreal and Toronto a small number of such men had joined informal volunteer units that kept alive a few embers of the military spirit.

View from Halifax Citadel showing Georges Island in foreground and McNabs Island in background.

At the beginning of the *Trent* crisis in 1861, active volunteers from the colonial militias amounted to only about 5,000 men, most of them virtually untrained. The possibility of war stimulated an expansion to 60,000 men. Volunteers responded enthusiastically, and were soon training under tough British sergeants. In Halifax, Joseph Howe said, "Half the members of the legislature . . . earned an appetite for breakfast in the drill room, and used to pass my windows on the coldest mornings with their rifles over their shoulders. The cracking of rifles is as common a sound as the note of the bobolink, and intercolonial shooting matches are becoming an irritation."

Tensions were renewed through the actions of the Fenian Brotherhood, a society of Irish nationalists who planned to strike a blow against Britain and indirectly create pressure to achieve their objective of an independent Ireland by attacking the British North American colonies. Most were recent immigrants to the U.S., fleeing the catastrophe of the Irish potato famine. Many had been soldiers in the Union Army. Their marching song went:

> *We are the Fenian Brotherhood, skilled in the arts of war,*
> *And we're going to fight for Ireland, the land we adore,*
> *Many battles we have won, along with the boys in blue,*
> *And we'll go and capture Canada, for we've nothing else to do.*

Between 1865 and 1871 the Fenians were allowed by the United States government to collect forces just inside the American border, from which they launched several raids into Canada. There was also threat to British Columbia; temporary defences were erected at Esquimalt dockyard and volunteer companies were raised, some of which would convert to units of the Canadian Militia after Confederation. On March 7, 1865 10,000 militia were called out in Canada. Ten days later a flurry of military preparations took place in Halifax in response to a report that a Fenian fleet was sailing from New York to attack the city. The report proved false, but not before rifles and ammunition were issued to the local militia.

The raiders had some success, but victories by the Canadian militia brought the incursions in Canada to an end. Thereafter, the American authorities took steps to prevent a renewal. The raids stimulated Canadian martial spirit by giving the militia a test of strength and valuable experience, achieved without the huge cost of a war.

The perceived threat of American aggression was a major factor in convincing the British colonies that they needed to unite for mutual protection. In 1867, at the request of the colonies of Canada, Nova Scotia, and New Brunswick, the British Parliament passed the *British North America Act*. It created a federation of the provinces of Quebec, Ontario, and the two former maritime

Rifled muzzle-loader gun, York Redoubt in the 1880s. These guns replaced those from the 1860s and had greater power, range, and accuracy.

colonies. The new Dominion, as it was styled in the *Act*, was internally self-governing, a first critical step in the journey to nationhood. The event failed to elicit any official recognition from the United States. Manitoba would join in 1870, British Columbia in 1871 and Prince Edward Island in 1873.

By this time the list of British–American irritants was a long one; the *Alabama* claims, the Fenian raids, the *Trent* incident, the San Juan Islands quarrel, and disputes over the east coast fisheries all continued to fester. Both countries had come to realize that tensions needed to be resolved to reduce the risk of an armed conflict that neither government wanted. As leader of the new country in which any war would be fought, peace was also the wish of Canadian Prime Minister Sir John A. Macdonald, but as yet the views of the Dominion carried little weight. In Confederation, Britain had retained its control over Canadian foreign policy and defence.

In 1871 a British–United States conference was convened to

settle the outstanding issues. The British delegation included Sir John, in recognition of his prime ministerial office. By accepting his inclusion under that title the Americans for the first time gave de facto recognition to the new country.

An agreement was hammered out which was formalized as the Treaty of Washington. The CSS *Alabama* claims were referred to an international tribunal meeting in Geneva. The Americans had claimed not only direct damages attributed to the ship's actions, but collateral damages amounting to the astonishing amount of $2,000,000,000 in 1871 dollars. Their strategy in making this demand was that in lieu of damages the British would cede British Columbia, Manitoba, and Nova Scotia to the United States. The tribunal refused to consider the collateral claims, but did award the United States $15,500,000 in direct damages. The British and Canadian counter-claim against the United States for costs and damages relating to the Fenian raids was disallowed. As well, Americans were given access to valuable fishing grounds in Canadian waters.

The tribunal referred the San Juan Islands dispute to arbitration by the German Emperor, who ruled in favour of the Americans. In retirement in Victoria, old Governor Sir James Douglas mourned to a daughter, "The Island of San Juan is gone at last. I cannot trust myself to speak about it and will be silent."

Not surprisingly, the Treaty of Washington was widely condemned in Canada. As the junior member of the British delegation Macdonald decided that he had to sign it, although he was far from content with its provisions. In side negotiations the Americans agreed to make a cash payment of $5.5 million for use of the fishing grounds and another $2.5 million for the Fenian damages claim. More importantly to Macdonald and to Canada in the long run, the British responded to Canadian discontent and promised a loan guarantee to finance the construction of the Canadian Pacific Railway (the CPR), a condition of British Columbia's entry into Confederation.

This would not be the last occasion when many Canadians would feel that their British colonial masters were all too ready to sacrifice Canadian interests in pursuit of better relations with the United States.

Another potential source of disagreement was the Monroe Doctrine. First enunciated in 1823, it was an American declaration that any effort by a European country to colonize or interfere in the affairs of the newly independent states anywhere in Latin America would be viewed as an act of aggression requiring American action. The doctrine was disregarded internationally. Though the British government never formally accepted the pronouncement, it did agree with its basic objective. At the time the Americans were too weak to enforce the Monroe Doctrine, but the British tacitly did, the power of the Royal Navy being unchallengeable.

***

Britain continued to have the growing responsibility of defending the new Dominion, a task made ever more difficult by the addition of new territory. In 1871 the Canadian government purchased Rupert's Land from the Hudson's Bay Company, thus acquiring the vast fur-trading area drained by all the rivers flowing into Hudson's Bay. It was an expensive burden of which many in Britain would have been glad to be relieved. With Confederation the Dominion appeared capable of making a greater contribution to its own security, and with great reluctance it slowly began to do so. But the continuing existence of British army bases on the two southern extremities of Canada gave the Royal Navy and Britain the necessary resources to operate on the high seas off American shores and to put military pressure on the United States, if that became necessary.

Canada instituted a standing army of regular soldiers, referred to as the permanent force. Initially very small, it consisted of an infantry school, a cavalry school, and two batteries of artillery. It was not intended to operate as an organized whole, its role being simply to provide training to the militia. A common militia system was applied to the whole country. A first annual appropriation of about $1,500,000 was voted, enough to support a force of 43,000 part-time volunteers, armed with the new Snider breech-loading rifles. Although much progress was made the system was still of doubtful effectiveness. The budget varied from year to year, and the limited funds failed to ensure a minimum standard of basic training. The best organized and most efficient units were located in the larger cities, the rural units generally being of much lower quality.

In 1870–71 Britain withdrew most of its Canadian garrisons from their inland military bases, and the fortresses of Quebec and Kingston and other military works were turned over to Canada. Nevertheless, Britain maintained its base and the regular garrison at the Halifax fortress. It was commanded by a lieutenant-general of the British army, "Commanding in Canada," and responsible to the War Office in London. Concurrently, peacetime command of the Canadian militia was always vested in another British officer, this time only a major-general, and responsible to the Canadian minister of militia.

In the event of war with the Americans the "Officer Commanding in Canada" was to move with his staff to the central provinces and assume full operational control of all troops in the country. In truth, "Canada was too large and Halifax was at one end," but the awkward arrangement lasted until 1900, when the Halifax commander's position was downgraded to the rank of colonel, always an artillery officer.

A Canada that now reached from the Atlantic to the Pacific contained just under four million people, compared to the thirty-five million of the United States. The traditional threat had been attack along the Great Lakes–St. Lawrence frontier. Thanks to the new country's extremely rapid expansion to the west coast the extended front now traversed twelve hundred miles of empty and indefensible woods and prairie from the head of Lake Superior to the Rockies. In the circumstances, British strategy continued to rely upon the enormously powerful Royal Navy, which at the time of Confederation maintained a strength greater than that of the next two naval powers combined, of which the United States was not one.

Fleets require bases. Accordingly, despite its general withdrawal, the imperial government continued to garrison the navy yards and fortifications at Esquimalt and Halifax.

In the event of war with Britain and the United States on opposite sides, a British fleet would be dispatched, powerful enough to win sea control in the western Atlantic. In the meantime, the fortress of Halifax would resist any American attack until the navy arrived. Operating from Halifax, the fleet would convoy reinforcement troops from Britain to central Canada and strangle American trade. In the same way, a defended base at Esquimalt would support a force that would protect British Columbia and its seaborne trade, while interdicting all shipping moving out of the American west coast. At the same time, Esquimalt was an asset for the British Navy whenever concerns arose regarding Russia and Japan and the need for defence against them. It was on this basis that the fortifications at Halifax and Esquimalt continued to be strengthened over most of the forty years following Confederation. Essentially, Canada would be defended against the United States by British sea power.

All depended on the defences of the fortresses protecting the naval bases. These rested on two pillars. First, the fortifications, embracing the coastal artillery emplacements, light and heavy guns and later searchlights sited to counter attack by enemy

Fort Charlotte on Georges Island. Once considered obsolete, it was rearmed and activated when war broke out in 1914.

vessels. Second, the soldiers of the garrison, both regulars and militia, manning the batteries, guarding against possible landings, and protecting vital points against sabotage. The two components constituted the fortresses, whose purpose was to defend the naval bases. Any protection rendered to the host cities was simply an unintended byproduct of that fundamental mission. In principle the navy was not to be involved in the protection of its own bases, liberating it for action on the high seas that would decide the outcome of a war.

Beginning in the mid-nineteenth century, coastal artillery entered a period of rapid and sweeping change. This is described in detail in the Appendix.

Rapid changes in technology began to shatter the time-tested principles of fortress design. Hitherto the defending batteries had mounted smooth-bore cannon, almost always firing solid shot of up to forty-two pounds weight, at ranges of up to two miles. A fleet of relatively flimsy wooden sailing vessels whose own guns could hardly reach the protected emplacements would be at a decisive disadvantage.

Regular British artillery firing field guns shortly before the British left in 1906,
having garrisoned the fortress since 1749.

Steam propulsion made the attacking vessels both faster and
more manoeuvrable, thus harder to hit. Armour-plated sides and
decks rendered solid shot less effective. Most importantly, larger
guns, built on new principles and firing explosive shells, allowed
ships to engage shore batteries from longer ranges and with
greater accuracy. Later, the possibility of attack by fast torpedo
boats became a new challenge for the defence.

During the thirty-year construction of the Halifax citadel,
maintenance of the supporting coastal batteries had been badly
neglected. Between 1862 and 1878 the British again virtually
rebuilt and re-equipped them in an attempt to keep up with the
rapidly changing technology. The last decades of the nineteenth
century witnessed two transformations of coastal defences
world wide. The first saw the transition from the smooth-bore
cannon to the rifled muzzle-loader, the second the advent of
the breech-loader.

In the first phase the old smooth-bores were replaced with
guns having rifled barrels. Rifling consisted in engraving spiral
grooves on the inside of the bore. These engaged with studs on

Royal Garrison Artillery unloading cargo in 1904.

the projectile, which was given a rapid spin as it travelled up the barrel, greatly improving range and accuracy. Round shot was replaced with conical projectiles of three calibres: 7-inch, 9-inch, and 10-inch, the guns weighing seven, twelve, and eighteen tons respectively. Unloading these enormous weapons from transports, hauling them from the wharves to the batteries, and mounting them in the emplacements was a huge challenge, ultimately mastered by the gunners and engineers of the garrisons.

Solid projectiles continued in use, especially for target practice, but gunpowder-filled shells predominated. The new rifled guns continued to be loaded charge-first through the muzzle. Accordingly, they were classified as rifled muzzle-loaders. On completion of the changeover the upgraded fortress of Halifax mounted sixty-one of these state-of-the-art weapons.

***

It was the Royal Navy that probably fired the first shots from a shore-mounted gun at Esquimalt. As described in the records of the Senior Naval Officer, a 32-pounder smooth-bore was landed to the spit off Coburg Peninsula. The target was the Fisgard Lighthouse, in which the keeper consented to remain. Round shot was accurately fired with charges up to six pounds, with no perceptible result. As a precaution, "The keeper had been instructed to show a flag should the firing in his opinion endanger the lighthouse."

But the smooth-bore era never really applied at Esquimalt. The first state-of-the-art fortifications consisted of four coast batteries, constructed in the summer of 1878, at a time of British–Russian tension over Turkey. The batteries were simple earthworks armed with rifled muzzle-loaders like those at Halifax. One was located at Finlayson Point, one at Victoria Point, one at Macaulay Point, and the third at Brothers Island.

To serve these batteries, a militia order on July 19, 1878, authorized the formation of the Victoria Battery of Garrison Artillery as a unit of the active militia. An advertisement in the *Daily Colonist* of February 17, 1878 read, "Persons desirous of enrolling themselves as a volunteer artillery corps are urgently requested to report themselves to the drill shed between 12 A.M and 2 P.M." Originally named The Victoria Battery of Coastal Artillery, on October 12, 1883 it became the 5th (British Columbia) Regiment of Canadian Garrison Artillery. Thus began the proud tradition of the Great War's 5th Regiment of Canadian Garrison Artillery, inherited and nurtured today by its successor, the militia's 5th Regiment Royal Canadian Artillery.

A feature of the regiment's training was the occasional sham fight against attacking warships, of course with blank ammunition. One such encounter is described in the following account from 1894:

*The ship attacked one of the batteries
at Beacon Hill, firing from some 2000 yards
distance, the guns replying with their fire. After
considerable shooting, which caused plenty of
noise and smoke, the land battery was supposed
to be silenced (signalled by the guns ceasing fire).
Boat loads of sailors from the ship then effected
a landing in grand style, and the gunners retired,
armed only with rifles, taking advantage of the
lay of the land to delay the enemy's advance. They
were finally driven back on their last defences,
which consisted of a long table abundantly
supplied with kegs of beer, bread and cheese,
where honourable terms were made with the
enemy.**

Hardly had these improvements been completed when technology rendered them obsolescent. In the 1880s and 1890s magazine rifles replaced single-shot personal weapons and the old black powder propellant was superseded by smokeless powder in guns of all calibres. Most importantly, advances in metallurgy and inventions such as the interrupted thread made it possible to open the hitherto solid breech for loading. The breech could then be shut, and was capable of withstanding the force of the exploding charge on firing.

The era of the breech-loader had arrived. Rifled muzzle-loaders firing shot or shell at a rate of one every one or two minutes gave place to breech-loaders firing rounds packing greater destructive power at the rate of several rounds per minute and to ever-increasing ranges. Breech-loaders were always rifled.

Because of their weights, the propelling charge and the

---

* From 5th (BC) Regiment, Canadian Garrison Artillery and Early Defences of the B.C. Coast: Historical Records, by Lieutenant-Colonel F.A. Robertson, 1925. Provided with the kind permission of the 5th (BC) Regiment.

Rifled muzzle-loader, York Redoubt in the 1880s. By 1914 there were no guns at Fort York, but the fire command post for the entire fortress was located there.

projectile still had to be loaded in sequence, thus heavier breech-loading guns still had a relatively slow rate of fire, unable to cope with raids by fast-moving torpedo craft. The new threat was met by the introduction of smaller, quick-firing guns. Quick-firers featured fixed ammunition, where the propelling charge and the projectile were light enough to be enclosed together within a single casing and loaded through the breech in a single movement, greatly increasing the rate of fire. The heaviest calibre of the true fixed-ammunition quick-firing gun was 4.7-inches, but, confusingly, some separate ammunition 6-inch breech-loaders were also referred to as "quick-firers."

Electricity began to be used for several purposes. At Halifax, Morse's electric telegraph took the place of the Prince's old mechanical system and was extended to Camperdown radio at the harbour mouth. The central node was Fort York, from which defence against sea attack was coordinated and command over the entire fortress was exercised.

Ives Point battery at the south end of McNabs Island.

The increased ranges of ships' guns meant that they had to be engaged and stopped much further from the inner harbour. Thus, there was a need for new, heavy batteries closer to the harbour entrances. On the other hand, the torpedo boat threat could be countered only by lighter, quick-firing weapons, mines, and searchlights within the harbour itself. Together, these requirements led to a parallel process of new construction, balanced by the decommissioning of old works whose locations no longer fit the circumstances.

In 1879 the British War Office commissioned a report on the defences of Esquimalt. The conclusion was that the fortress was indefensible against a major American attack. Nevertheless, with improvements it would be possible to repel American raids, and also attacks by any other power, meaning Russia at that time, but later Japan. (Germany was not yet a factor.) The cost of doing so was very large, and a garrison of thirteen hundred troops would be required thereafter.

From the navy's strategic perspective, Halifax remained one of the most important bases in the Empire. Thus the British

Mobile component of Canadian Garrison Artillery after the departure of the British. These field guns were used to defend the fortresses against attack from the rear.

simply decided at different times how the fortress was to be modernized, and the army implemented the necessary improvements. All funding came from the British treasury, always to the very significant economic benefit of the local area. The Canadian government was in no way involved. However, regarding Esquimalt, the Royal Navy did not consider that heavy expenditure was justified by the strategic value of the base. Unless Canada would agree to a cost-sharing arrangement nothing would be done. Trying to achieve agreement on that basis would result in frustrating delays.

In 1885 the Canadian government accepted in principle an imperial proposal that Canada should build the emplacements and provide the garrison. For its part, the British would furnish the armament, plus expert construction and operating assistance. The British would pay about 60 per cent of the fixed costs, with Canada covering the ongoing expenses. The defence was to consist of six mobile artillery pieces and six machine guns, plus 6-inch batteries at Rodd Hill on the southern side of Esquimalt harbour and at Macaulay Point at the entrance to Victoria harbour. Finally, to cover the outer approaches, a longer range battery of four high-angled 9-inch rifled muzzle-loaders was to be emplaced at Signal Hill.

As at Halifax, a submarine minefield was to be laid on the bottom across the entrance to the harbour, and searchlights were positioned

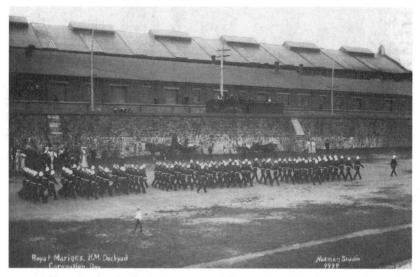

A specially trained unit of Royal Marine Artillery manned the batteries and sub-marine mines at Esquimalt in the last years of the British Garrison.

as a counter to night raids. (Although controlled minefields were laid in both harbours they were eliminated by 1914 and did not appear in the defence schemes then.)

But acceptance in principle did not entail effective action, as the Canadian government found new reasons to hesitate. The fixed cost estimates escalated, always an important consideration. But the main problem was the garrison. A and B Batteries at Quebec and Kingston were the only artillery units in the regular force. Each provided a detachment to form C Battery and a school of artillery, established first in a Victoria exhibition building and then at Work Point Barracks. A main role of C Battery was to train the militia, but poor living conditions and high local wages led to rates of desertion that eventually crippled the unit. Nor did it possess the expertise to operate the sophisticated disappearing 6-inch guns or the remotely controlled minefield.

Therefore, in 1888 the British amended their 1885 proposal to

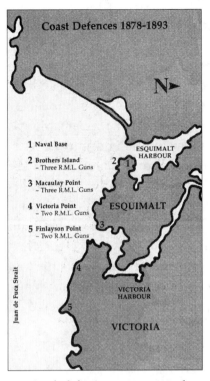

Esquimalt defences 1878 to 1893, the rifled muzzle-loader era.

provide regular Royal Marine Artillery gunners and submarine mine experts to the garrison, to be paid for by Canada. Still there was no agreement.

Canadian politics would eventually decide the issue. The federal government was sensitive to pressure from a virtually defenceless British Columbia. Apart from protecting the base, coastal defences at Esquimalt would shield the Vancouver area and the important coal port of Nanaimo from attack through the Strait of Juan de Fuca. Writing in 1892, Major-General Ivor J.C. Herbert, the British officer commanding the Canadian militia, observed:

The only argument I have found effective with the government is the possible withdrawal of the naval station from Esquimalt. That is a very vulnerable point as no government would risk the loss of popularity which such withdrawal would entail . . . the removal of the naval station and the money it brings into British Columbia would send all these constituencies over to the opposition. Moreover it would affect [Finance Minister] Mr. Foster's operations by lowering the confidence in England as to Canadian stability.

In 1893 a new cost-sharing formula was agreed upon. In August of that year the first Royal Marine Artillery detachment took over Work Point Barracks from C Battery. The Marine Artillery was the cream of the corps of Royal Marines, and the detachment had received additional special training to operate the controlled minefield. Possibly no other regular unit was so effective in training the Canadian militia and imparting its standard of discipline and professionalism, a standard that the militia's 5th Garrison Artillery would maintain in the years before the war. A Royal Engineer major supervised the demolition of the 1878 earthworks and the construction of the Rodd Hill and Macaulay Point forts. By the end of 1897 the guns had been mounted on the finished works. The planned battery of 9.2-inch rifled muzzle-loaders was not completed, and for many years the components of the huge weapons were left scattered on Signal Hill.

Esquimalt thus joined the worldwide network of British fortresses, conforming generally to the Halifax model. In wartime, the core of British regulars and the mobilized militia would both come under the command of the British officer commanding the Royal Marine Artillery, as would the hundred-man reinforcement of regular-force garrison artillery from the east that Canada was committed to provide.

Such was the general state of the fortifications after the final upgrade. To complete the picture, we must turn from the forts and batteries to the second pillar of fortress defence, the garrisons.

Despite constant changes in potential enemies, and the ever more rapid evolution of coastal artillery, the general outlines of fortress garrisons remained remarkably similar for centuries. Under British control battalions of regular infantry rotated through Halifax, defended vital points and prepared to operate in the open field against an attack by land. Coastal forts and batteries outside the United Kingdom were manned by travelling

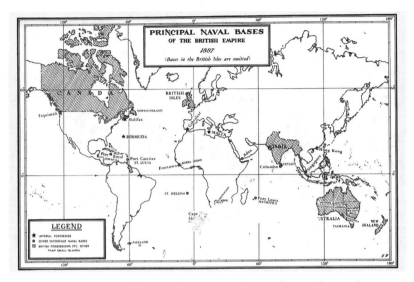

Principal naval bases of the British Empire in 1887. These widespread ports enabled the Royal Navy to exert its power on a worldwide basis.

companies of the Royal Garrison Artillery. Working closely with the artillery, Royal Engineers improved and maintained the fabric of the defences. Each artillery company spent three or four years in one garrison, before being relieved and moving on to another. In the western Atlantic, the usual rotation was a Caribbean Island, then Bermuda, then Halifax, and home.

As we have seen, Esquimalt departed from this pattern in that the Royal Marine Artillery took the place of the Royal Garrison Artillery. As well, no British army infantry battalions were ever stationed there. At this time also the local militia was far below the strength of its counterpart in Halifax.

***

In 1891, Major-General Herbert instituted significant reforms in the regular force. A full field battery was established at Kingston, and a partial field battery and garrison artillery at Quebec, the two

Princess Louise Fusiliers on the prairie during the North-West Rebellion of 1885.

locations together forming the Regiment of Canadian Artillery. The cavalry and mounted infantry schools were amalgamated into the Regiment of Canadian Dragoons, and four infantry companies were combined to form the Royal Canadian Regiment of Infantry. In 1894 all four trained as a unit for the first time, signalling an increased emphasis on tactical operations.

The first Riel Rebellion occurred in Manitoba in 1870. British regulars and Canadian militia marched overland on the Red River Trail from the head of Lake Superior and put it down without bloodshed. However, when in 1885 the second Riel Rebellion broke out in the Northwest Territories the British had gone and it would be up to Canadian troops to suppress it.

Over three hundred regular soldiers served in the rebellion, but success would depend on the militia. Most city units mobilized with great rapidity and enthusiasm. They made a harrowing winter journey to the west, thanks largely to the still-building Canadian Pacific Railway. Around the north shore of Lake Superior were large unfinished gaps, which the shivering men crossed in open sleighs or marching on the frozen surface of the lake.

Once in the field the force had severe logistic problems, and

Band and troops of the British Garrison marching through Point Pleasant Park.

it was revealed that even in these relatively effective units some men lacked basic small-arms training. In several engagements the Métis and Natives more than held their own. The British commander, Major-General Frederick Middleton, had little confidence in the troops and was reluctant to commit them to serious action. Morale naturally faltered. But at the Métis capital of Batoche the militia more or less took things into its own hands, with a spontaneous attack that overran the defences and led to the capture of Riel. The returning troops received an enthusiastic welcome in their home communities.

The volunteer militia was simply not large enough. In a country with over one million men of military age paper strength was never over sixty thousand, and in a given year sometimes as few as forty thousand actually received training. Many men passed through the units, but no attempt was made to keep track of them afterwards. The arrangements and facilities for mobilization barely sufficed for the limited needs of the Rebellion, and would have proved quite inadequate in the event of a general mobilization.

For more than a hundred years British garrisons had helped

*Halifax Rifles Non-commissioned Officers during the North-West Rebellion of
1885.*

to train the militia, many units of which were co-located with the
regulars. The relationship continued at Halifax and Esquimalt.
But with the departure of the garrisons from central Canada in
1871–72 the militia there lost what had been an invaluable training and mentoring asset, although a lasting spirit of trust and
camaraderie between British regulars and Canadian militia never
emerged.

At Halifax, where the British still remained, an officer of the
Halifax Rifles wrote:

> . . . *the impression seems general in militia
> circles in other parts of the Dominion that great
> advantages are derived from corps being in a city
> garrisoned by regular troops, but unfortunately
> this is not the case, as long experience has proven.
> Professionals, whether in military matters or in
> cricket or baseball matches, do not look on those*

*who serve either for honour or pleasure, with a
kindly eye, and although the Imperial troops in
Halifax have ever been friendly to the local forces
there had not for years been any cordiality or
fraternal feelings between them.*

After the departure of the British it might have been expected
that things would be different in central Canada now that regulars and militia were both Canadian. In fact, little changed. As
under the British regime, training went on, always limited by
lack of funds, but the full-time and part-time forces remained
distinct in other ways.

There was an emotional aspect to the cleavage. In the course
of the nineteenth century there grew up what has been called the
"militia myth." Justly proud of their record in 1812, the North-
West Rebellion and the Fenian raids, many of the militia believed
that when the chips were down the enterprising citizen soldier
was equal or even superior to a robotic regular. Fairly or unfairly,
it was believed that the typical regular soldier, paid at the rate of
50 cents a day, was little more than a refugee from the gutter. The
regular officers as a group were perceived as men who could not
succeed in the competitive civilian world, preferring the ordered
military life and the convivial society of the mess. Sam Hughes, a
future minister of militia and defence, opined that "the regulars
were all right for police purposes in time of peace, but beyond
that they are an injury to the Nation."

Patronage was rife within both the militia and the regular
force, and many officers of both branches were far from properly
qualified. As late as 1913 a British officer seconded to the regular
garrison artillery at Esquimalt's Work Point Barracks could write,

*I found the poor old barracks in a
pitiful condition, chiefly owing to the entire*

*incompetency of Colonel Roy the District Officer
Commanding. Being neither a soldier nor a
gentleman does not know how to deal with the
questions that arise and are not legislated for by
King's Regulations . . . There is one, Major J.E.
Mills, RCGA, who has misappropriated some
thousands of canteen and company funds, and
this not for the first time, as he did the same thing
in Kingston. He has put about $1500 of the Golf
Club funds in his own pocket likewise. The Senior
Naval Officer has now taken the matter up with
the DOC but can get no satisfaction, as word has
come from Ottawa that Mills is not to be court-
martialed, but is to be given a staff appointment
at Kingston. As the whole countryside knows
of his misdoings you may imagine the harm
this action of Sam Hughes will do to the Militia
Department. The very name "Barracks" stinks
in the land, which comes very hard on those
officers who are innocent. Moreover, such political
whitewashing of an officer is not conducive to
good order and military discipline. Apparently
the father, Dr. Mills of Ottawa, is a good friend of
Sam's who is covering this criminal's retreat . . .*

The Royal Military College of Canada was founded in 1876, and a slow trickle of committed graduates emerged to join both the regulars and the militia. Deadwood was gradually weeded out, the competence of the permanent officer corps steadily improved, but patronage remained a serious problem. Money was at the heart of the matter. Defence funding was very limited, and in the eyes of the militia any funds directed to the regular or to the Royal Military College were in effect stolen from the citizen soldiers, the real defenders of the Dominion.

The decades after Confederation saw sweeping changes in both international affairs and Canadian attitudes. For Canada the outstanding features were the rise of a spirit of Canadian nationalism, the gradual improvement in British–American relations and the emergence of Germany and Japan as world powers. The interplay among them had a profound effect on the question of national defence, and a direct impact on the Victoria and Halifax fortresses. In the last twenty years before the Great War events would unfold against this changing background.

In the late 1880s the Dominion went through a period of agonizing self-doubt, the product of a long depression, the apparent failure of economic policy, and the threat to national unity triggered by the execution of Louis Riel over the strenuous objections of Quebec. It was in this climate that an organized movement in favour of imperial consolidation took root. Spearheaded by the Imperial Federation League, it had its counterparts in Britain and other parts of the Empire, all of whom co-operated in promoting the vision. But only Canada, with its expansionist neighbour, saw British defence support as the primary motivation for closer imperial ties.

The term "imperialism" had a specific meaning in this context. The aim of the Imperial Federation League was to integrate the component parts of the Empire through economic, constitutional and military arrangements, leading to imperial unity or imperial federation. Its Canadian proponents believed that only by acquiring influence within this framework could the country achieve the national status to which it aspired. It may have been best expressed by the future prime minister, Robert Borden, when he said, "I am an imperialist because I don't want to be a colonial." Politically, the Conservative Party, with its Ontario base, was most likely to favour the imperial approach.

The nationalist opponents to the imperialist approach

Royal Navy ships in Esquimalt harbour 1870.

espoused a contrary view. Often referred to as Canada Firsters, they believed that Canada's international stature would best be promoted by concentrating on internal development, unity, and self-government. Conversely, entanglement in wider organizations where the interests of others might prevail was to be strictly avoided. The bitter and divisive conflict between these two visions was a dominant theme in the decades preceding the World War. The nationalist view was centred in but not confined to Quebec and was closest to the policy of the Liberal Party.

Although British–American relations were steadily improving, friction was by no means eliminated. In 1895 a dispute arose over the boundary between Venezuela and British Guiana; the area in question was believed to be rich in gold. The Venezuelans sought American support. Invoking the Monroe Doctrine, President Grover Cleveland threatened Britain with strong action unless it agreed to put the dispute to arbitration, stating that "The United States is practically sovereign on this continent, and its fiat is law . . ." In the same letter occurred the phrase "any permanent political union between an European and an American state is unnatural and inexpedient."

After some delay British Prime Minister Lord Salisbury replied in a rather patronizing manner that the Doctrine had no basis in international law, and rejected the implication that Canada did not have the right to remain within the British Empire. The press and public on both sides of the Atlantic erupted in anger, and for a time war seemed imminent.

At the time the Royal Navy had fifty-five battleships, the American navy just three. It was obvious that the only possible American strategy would be the traditional one, an invasion of Canada. In the Dominion the issue produced a resurgence of anti-American feeling, coupled with astonishment and a determination to defend the country.

Unfortunately, the means to do so no longer existed. British land forces had gone, except at Halifax and Esquimalt, and Canada's regular army was minuscule. Along the frontier the protective forests had largely been cleared. The newly arrived British commander General Herbert was astonished to learn that there was no up-to-date anti-invasion plan. Above all, the efficiency and strength of the militia had deteriorated to an all-time low.

Fortunately cooler heads prevailed. Influential people on both sides of the Atlantic were soon writing to the press and lobbying politicians, arguing that war between kindred nations sharing the same values would be a travesty. The same letters were often printed by newspapers in both Britain and the United States. The crisis ended when the president declared that war would be both an absurdity and a crime. The dispute was eventually arbitrated under American auspices. But the implicit threat by the United States government against Canada, and its assertion that Canada was not free to make decisions about its constitution and political future independent of the United States, had been countered. The weight of the Royal Navy and its capacity to operate against the United States had been felt.

The 1900 Boxer Rebellion in China saw British and American troops fighting side by side for the first time since the Seven Years' War. Further continental expansion having been virtually ruled out by the growth of Mexico and Canada, a new field was needed for the realization of Manifest Destiny. In 1898 the Americans won their last war with Spain, acquiring Puerto Rico and the Philippines, thus becoming a colonial power like the European countries which they had previously criticized. Thenceforth the Caribbean was their area of principal interest. Still rivals in many respects, Britain and the United States increasingly found that their interests coincided rather than conflicted. The risk of a serious breach between them was becoming vanishingly small. Realistically, Canada could hardly be seen as their potential battleground.

The original boundary between Russian possessions and British territory had never been clearly described or surveyed. In 1896 gold was discovered on Klondike Creek near Dawson City in the Yukon. Word did not reach the outside world until the next year, triggering a massive rush of hopeful prospectors from all over North America and the world. Until an all-Canadian overland route was completed the only access to the diggings was through American ports in the Alaska Panhandle. A few miles inland was what Canada considered to be the boundary, disputed by the Americans. Customs posts of each country jostled for position, and the Americans were alleged to be making Canadian access as inconvenient as possible.

The Northwest Mounted Police were reinforced and brought law and order to the town and diggings. But when Dawson ran short of provisions the Americans announced a plan to send a relief expedition of two hundred armed soldiers to the assistance of the supposedly starving miners, a significant majority of whom were Americans. This menacing combination could not be ignored. Ever wary, the Canadian government organized the Yukon Field Force of 203 officers and men of the permanent army, with two Maxim machine guns and two 7-pounder artillery pieces. Rushed from central Canada to Vancouver on the Canadian Pacific Railroad, they travelled by steamer to Wrangell, Alaska, and thence up the Stikine River and overland to Dawson, a wilderness march of incredible difficulty. With no reason given, the proposed American relief expedition was cancelled. The Yukon remained Canadian. The permanent force had its uses after all.

However, in the broader sense the country was virtually defenceless unless Britain intervened militarily, an eventuality that seemed less probable year by year. The Admiralty was most hesitant. The growing German threat steadily reduced the possibility that a powerful force could be detached from the Home Fleet to fight on the other side of the Atlantic. The British army, on the other hand, remained committed. The position as seen by the army-dominated Colonial Defence Committee was summed up as follows:

> . . . *the defence of her long frontiers cannot be left to Canada unaided, and so long as it is her free wish to remain a member of the Empire she must be and she will be supported with the whole force at our disposal. To state this proposition is of course to proclaim the reciprocal obligation of the Dominion.*

The last sentence may hold the key to the British army's position. In the future, a reversal of the direction of military support might some day become desirable.

The need for Canada to revitalize the militia was too blatant to be ignored. Wilfrid Laurier's victory in the election of 1896 was partly due to public disgust at the state to which it had been reduced. The new Liberal minister of militia was Dr. Frederick Borden, cousin of the leader of the Conservative Party. A native of the Annapolis Valley, he had served for thirty years as a militia medical officer, was well aware of its problems, and was popular with other militia officers. Perhaps his biggest advantage was that he would have over fifteen years in a ministerial portfolio that had been a revolving door under his predecessors.

Beginning in 1896 a number of improvements were carried out in quick succession. Annual training camps were reinstituted, fifty-two unit commanders were retired, the commandant of the Royal Military College was replaced, and an exchange programme between British and Canadian forces was implemented. Borden relied heavily for policy advice and execution on Colonel P.H.N. Lake, the British quartermaster-general at Militia Headquarters. Married to a Canadian, he was liked and trusted by Canadians, unlike many senior British officers. In 1904 he would become the first Chief of the Canadian General Staff.

A major deficiency was remedied in 1898 when a Committee on Canadian Defence was brought into being, a precondition for the development of emergency plans and organization. It was made up of military experts and Minister of Militia Borden. As it was deliberating, Major-General E.T.H. Hutton, British commander in Canada, wrote a scathing report, stating that Canada's force formed "not an army . . . but a collection of military units without cohesion, without staff, and without those military departments by which an army is moved, fed or ministered to in sickness." The Committee came to much the same conclusions, expressed in more sober style.

Hutton showed much more energy than many of his predecessors, and through numerous inspections made himself a great deal better informed. His knowledge of detail and appreciation of the real needs of the force impressed the militia, which responded with enthusiasm. He also worked hard to improve the pay and professionalism of the regular force, and attempted to make its officers pensionable. However, that initiative died when the anti-regular-forces Sam Hughes argued in the Commons ". . . let these fellows just save up their money"; this at a time when their pay was one-third that of their American counterparts and half that of the British. Hutton greatly improved the quality of training at summer camps, but to his fury his efforts to eliminate political patronage in both the regular force and the militia were only partially successful.

***

In 1903 the government established a professional headquarters staff organized on the British model, headed by a Chief of the General Staff who reported through the Militia Council to the minister. The incumbent thus assumed the role previously assigned to the General Officer Commanding British troops in Canada, an arrangement that no longer seemed consistent with Canadian development and growing nationalism. Transport and stores that had previously been very badly managed by civilian staff were transferred to the new Army Service Corps, and a medical director general was appointed. Training schools and armouries were built, and within the limitations of the budget due attention was paid to the acquisition of modern arms and equipment. This included the adoption of the .303 calibre Lee-Enfield rifle, but, unfortunately, that was not the weapon with which the Canadian Expeditionary Force would go to war in 1914.

At the Colonial Conference of 1897 the idea had first been raised that the colonies might render Britain military support, not only in defending their own territories, but by directly assisting Britain in conflicts elsewhere in the Empire; the "reciprocal obligation" enunciated by the Colonial Defence Committee. A case in point soon arose.

The discovery of gold and diamonds in massive quantities in the republics of the Orange Free State and Transvaal triggered an influx of British subjects who soon outnumbered the Boer population. Tensions escalated as the Boer governments imposed what were seen as undemocratic restrictions on the outlanders. The German Emperor aggravated the situation by sending a supportive telegram to Paul Krueger, the Free State President, together with modern rifles and artillery. War broke out between these independent African states controlled by European settlers and the British government in 1899. At the time the United States was busy quelling its own rebellion in the Philippines, and hardly in a position to object to British action in southern Africa.

Liberal Prime Minister Sir Wilfrid Laurier was opposed to assisting Britain militarily in a conflict that was of no concern to Canada. Indeed, many in Quebec identified with the Boers as a people like themselves, victims of British colonialism. But behind the scenes the Colonial Office in London and Governor General Lord Minto conspired with General Hutton to draw up plans for an expeditionary force. When they were revealed the British government blandly thanked Canada for its offer of assistance, and there was intense pressure from Canadian imperialists to follow through. Another factor in Laurier's eventual approval was the hope that Canada would be rewarded by British support in the Alaska boundary dispute.

A special volunteer 2nd Battalion of the Royal Canadian Regiment was raised, and by the end of November it was in Cape Town. Meanwhile, militia of the Canadian Garrison Artillery had temporarily taken over defence of the Halifax fortress from the British troops, who sailed for the theatre of war. Canadian government pressure forced the recall of General Hutton, who coincidentally later commanded the British brigade in South

Canadian Mounted Rifles parading through Halifax en route to the Boer War.

Africa to which the Canadians were attached. Outside Quebec the country's participation was generally supported. When in 1900 the Canadian Mounted Rifles boarded their transport in Halifax, the whole city turned out to see them off. Canadian troops were deemed to have performed well in several actions, most particularly at Paardeberg, where they were instrumental in forcing the surrender of the Boer General Piet Cronjé.

The British regarrisoned Halifax after the war. Plagued by indiscipline, the militia garrison had not been an impressive substitute.

After years of inconclusive and often acrimonious discussion the Alaska boundary dispute came to a head. The issue affected Canada directly but was in itself of no concern to Britain. Nevertheless, the mother country continued to be responsible for colonial foreign policy and therefore played a leading role in negotiating the settlement.

In 1903 the Hay–Herbert Treaty between the United States and Great Britain established a bilateral Joint Commission to settle the issue. The original concept was that there were to be six commissioners (three judges from each side) and an independent arbitrator. Under pressure the British finally agreed to the American senate's demands that there be no arbitrator and that the American commissioners be politicians, not judges. Of the British commissioners two were Canadian and the third a British judge.

The Canadian government was aware that its case was questionable but had allowed the public to believe that with British support it was winnable, a rare instance of nationalism and imperialism acting in concert. Naturally the politically-driven American commissioners were solidly behind the American claim. The British Foreign Office put great pressure on the British judge, under the threat that without a favourable decision the Americans would simply occupy the whole of the disputed area.

The upshot was that the British commissioner voted with the Americans. Canadian reaction was vitriolic, against the British commissioner and even more against the British government, upon whom Laurier succeeded in deflecting the blame. From the Canadian standpoint the interests of the Dominion had once again been sacrificed on the altar of good British–American relations. President Theodore Roosevelt's comments after the award appeared to confirm that judgement. The insult was all the more galling since Canada's assistance and sacrifices in the Boer War seemed to have counted for nothing.

A wry joke of the time had a Canadian geography teacher asking a student to describe Canada. The student's answer: "Canada is that part of North America that the Americans have not yet decided that they need."

Deeply felt resentment lingered, but for most Canadians the setback was soon eclipsed by their pride in the country's rapid economic and population growth, captured in Laurier's declaration that the twentieth century would belong to Canada. The expansion was due in large part to a spectacular influx of immigrants, mostly to the still-empty prairie provinces. In *Halifax, Warden of the North,* Thomas Raddall tells of wistful Haligonians watching immigrants in their thousands disembark in their city, only to board the trains that would speed them to the cheap and fertile western lands.

With eyes turned inward, the majority of Canadians had little knowledge and less interest in quarrels that appeared both obscure and far away. Even the better-informed government was able to contemplate the geopolitical situation without undue alarm. But it would not be long before peaceful and remote Canada would be caught up in the march of events.

CHAPTER THREE
Rumours of War, 1906–1914

In the Alaska boundary affair Britain acted in her own interests, a characteristic of all nations when side issues are stripped away. At the turn of the twentieth century she was involved in disputes with Russia, France, and Japan. In the background Germany was emerging as a potential naval rival. Relative to other nations Britain's power was in decline. Little wonder that she made every effort to eliminate any risk from the United States.

Great Britain made no pretensions to be a military power. Her long-service volunteer army was mainly deployed in the colonies, and was laughably small in relation to the huge conscription-based armies of Germany and other continental powers. But since the end of the Napoleonic wars in 1818 Britain had maintained at great expense the largest navy in the world to protect the seaborne trade on which national prosperity and even the ability to feed her population entirely depended. Her army was not a threat to anyone, but as an island nation her navy made her invulnerable to attack. There were continental wars and minor

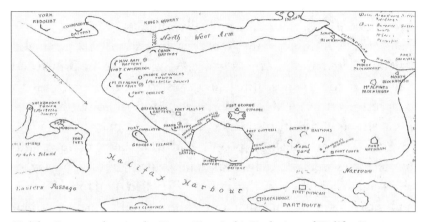

Halifax Fortress, drawing by Harry Piers in his Evolution of Halifax Fortress 1749 to 1928. *It shows all the defensive works active at one time or another up to and including WWI. Piers was the curator of the provincial museum.*

colonial conflicts, but in general the strategic balance ensured a period of world peace for more than fifty years.

But in the later nineteenth century the world's political and strategic realities began to change in ways that seemed sure to upset the balance. Canada had no influence on this transition, but Britain began to be increasingly affected, and her ever more dangerous situation was to involve the Dominion in new defence challenges.

After centuries of deliberate isolation Japan set about an urgent program of modernization. Based on a rapidly industrializing economy, the armed forces were transformed into efficient weapons. To some extent the army was modelled on the German example, and the navy on that of Great Britain, an island nation like Japan itself. Advisors from the respective countries made valuable contributions in the early stages, but soon the Japanese had no need of mentors.

In 1895 China was defeated in a short war that confirmed Japan as the rising naval power in the Pacific. It was apparent to the British that reinforcing their Far East fleet would commit them to a regional naval race they probably could not win. But Japan's main rival was Russia, rather than Britain, and in 1902 Japan and Britain entered into a formal alliance. At one stroke the British had neutralized the Japanese threat and enlisted them as a Far Eastern counterweight to the Russians. The stage was set for a transfer of naval strength to British waters if it should become necessary.

The German-speaking people had long been divided into numerous sovereign kingdoms and principalities. They were allies against France in the Franco–Prussian War of 1870–71, and victory resulted in their unification within a new German Empire, of which the Prussian king was crowned emperor, or "kaiser." The conquered areas of Alsace and Lorraine were embodied in the Empire, awakening a bitter thirst for revenge in the French nation, and sowing the seeds of a renewed conflict.

The German army was the second-largest in Europe, after Russia's, and by a long way the best trained and most efficient. At the age of eighteen every fit German male underwent a two-year period of military service, afterwards passing into the ever-growing reserve. Mustering seven hundred thousand men in peacetime, the standing army would be more than quadrupled on mobilization, which would be faster in Germany than any-where else. Developed over generations, the German general staff system ensured that its strategic and tactical doctrine was in the forefront of military thinking.

For German nationalists this was not enough. A latecomer to the wave of colonialism in the last half of the nineteenth century, by the early twentieth Germany's overseas possessions were negligible in comparison with those of Britain, France, and the United States, or even with those of Belgium, Portugal, and the Netherlands. She lacked her "place in the sun." Not incidentally, she also lacked a navy.

Kaiser Wilhelm II came to the throne in 1888. As a result of a birth accident he had a withered left arm, which he always attempted to conceal. In 1890 he dismissed his father's cautious chancellor, Otto von Bismarck, and became a champion of the nationalist wave sweeping Germany.

On his mother's side he was a grandson of Queen Victoria. During one of his frequent boyhood visits he had been spellbound with wonder on witnessing a review of the massed British fleet. He subsequently stated, "Then there arose in me the wish to build ships of my own like these some day, and when I was grown up to possess as fine a navy as the English."

Wilhelm's personal feelings carried weight, but for Germany the underlying impetus was the coupling of nationalism with industrial might. Beginning in 1898 a series of navy bills was passed by the Reichstag to finance a fleet of forty-one battleships that would make the German navy second to none. She soon overtook France as the second-largest naval power. The 1900 act was accompanied by the statement, "Germany must have a battle fleet so strong that even for the adversary with the strongest sea power a war against it would involve such dangers as to imperil his position in the world." This open statement of intent could only be construed as a threat. The German policy struck at the very existence of Great Britain, and by extension her colonies and empire. Survival depended on maintaining a decisive naval superiority.

Thus, as the risk of conflict with the United States was declining for Britain, Germany emerged as an ever more threatening potential enemy. In the event of conflict between them both Esquimalt and especially Halifax would play a role. Even as Britain withdrew her naval and military forces to the homeland, she continued to strengthen the fixed defences of the Canadian dockyard ports for reuse in an emergency.

In the early years of the twentieth century navies were actively experimenting with aircraft, submarines, and the new torpedo. But the decisive factor remained the battleship, successor to the sailing ship of the line, which had been the symbol of naval power for centuries. Heavily armoured, steam driven, with guns of ever-increasing power, battleship fleets were expected to face each other in a great battle which would decide the outcome of any war between Germany and Britain.

Based in harbours on the North Sea coast, the German High Seas Fleet could prepare a sortie at maximum strength at a time of its own choosing. Unpredictable accidents, strategic detachments, and periodic repairs meant that on any given day Britain's Grand Fleet could not be counted upon to be at its full strength. Thus, a simple superiority of numbers was not enough. Britain must have a sufficient margin of battleships in home waters to guarantee victory even in the most unfavourable circumstances.

As long ago as 1865 the British government had empowered its overseas possessions to raise local naval forces, with little response. The colonies continued to be spared the need to defend their maritime interests. But with her resources strained to the limit the British government finally sought assistance from its self-governing dependencies Canada, New Zealand, Australia, and South Africa. They were developing quickly and gradually casting off their colonial heritage, but from the British standpoint it was obvious that they remained just as dependent as Britain herself on the strength of the Royal Navy.

In face of the German menace France and Britain concluded the Dual Entente of 1904, an understanding that war between them was to be avoided at all costs. This allowed the Admiralty to draw down naval strength in the Mediterranean in order to reinforce the Home Fleet. As yet there was no formal alliance to strengthen the Dual Entente, but by 1906 secret talks were under way between the French and British militaries. One year later Russia joined the two countries in the Triple Entente, a counterweight to the Triple Alliance of Italy, Germany, and Austria-Hungary.

The 1902 Colonial Conference in London established a Committee of Imperial Defence to coordinate the Empire's response to the increasing international tension. The Admiralty requested the dominions to make financial contributions to ensure that Britain could keep pace in the naval race with Germany. Prime Minister Sir Wilfrid Laurier took the position that as an independent nation, albeit within the Empire, it would be inconsistent for Canada to support this centralist proposal. No agreement was reached, but for the first time Canada seemed willing to consider some form of naval defence.

Not for the last time Canada was torn by a controversy driven by developments over which she had no influence. The British request brought into sharp focus the contending nationalist and imperialist views of Canada's future. At the extreme wing of Laurier's Liberal Party the most avid nationalists stood for having no navy at all, to avoid becoming entangled in British foreign and defence policy. At the other extreme, mainly in Sir Robert Borden's Conservative Party, those who remained totally committed to the Empire advocated a substantial Canadian financial contribution to the Royal Navy. Not unnaturally, this was the policy that the British themselves strongly preferred.

A small step was taken when the Canadian Government Ship *Canada* was built to enforce fisheries regulations on the east coast. She was manned by a uniformed crew and heavily armed, a small warship by any other name. The Marine Service received a new commander, retired Rear-Admiral Charles E. Kingsmill, Royal Navy.

Faced with ever-growing German naval power, Britain responded by increasing her own building program to maintain the vital margin of battleship superiority. As a further measure, the strength of overseas fleets and squadrons was reduced, the surplus vessels being concentrated in home waters. The 1902 alliance with Japan was validated in 1905 when the Russian Far East Fleet was destroyed by Admiral Togo at the Battle of Tsushima. With her ally Japan supreme in the Pacific, the

Royal Navy disbanded its squadron at Esquimalt and reduced its strength there to two outdated vessels. The North America and West Indies Station was reduced from fourteen vessels to three. In all, the number of ships in overseas stations declined from 160 to 76; the most modern ships were added to the fleets in British home waters.

The strategic value of Halifax and Esquimalt continued to be a matter of contentious debate by the Colonial Defence Committee, revolving around whether war with United States could be disregarded as a possibility. Hong Kong was now the main British base in the Pacific, and a fleet based there could defend Canada's west coast against powers other than the Americans just as well as if it had been based in Esquimalt. In 1903 the Colonial Defence Committee recommended, and the British government agreed, that Esquimalt should no longer be maintained as a defended port. The economic impact of such a withdrawal on the Victoria area, however, would have raised political problems for the Laurier government. It therefore secured the transfer of seventy-nine men of the departing British garrison to Canadian service, and a similar transfer occurred in Halifax. Thus, skeleton forces of Canadian regular-force garrison artillery and engineers came into being on both coasts, of course in the hope that Canadians would also join the new national units.

The Committee of Imperial Defence took a different view with regard to Halifax. In a war with the Americans it considered that most of Canada could not be defended, but that the fortress of Halifax was capable of prolonged resistance even if local control of the sea were to be temporarily lost. In the years before the War defence plans continued to be based on this premise, and the required garrison was actually elevated to a level sufficient to resist an attack by ten thousand to fifteen thousand invaders.

***

Royal Canadian regiment guard at Wellington Barracks. This regular force Canadian battalion replaced the British Garrison Infantry in 1906.

The Canadian government received another unmistakable signal that the world was changing in ways that could not be ignored. It was informed that the much-reduced North America and West Indies Squadron of the Royal Navy would no longer require its Halifax base, except in an emergency. In such an event reinforcements would be dispatched to Halifax, but even that would happen only if the units were not otherwise occupied in home waters. The Esquimalt and Halifax dockyards would be transferred to the Dominion, and the British garrisons would be withdrawn.

On November 15, 1905, the first party of British Garrison Artillery left Halifax for home. On December 3, 1906, the Canadian Department of Militia and Defence took over Wellington Barracks for the battalion of the Royal Canadian Regiment that would be the sole regular infantry unit in the garrison. The last British troops left Halifax in February and Esquimalt in May 1906, having in the case of Halifax garrisoned the fortress for 175 years, and leaving the forts, batteries, and barracks on both coasts in excellent condition. Despite the turnover the British continued to review fortress mobilization schemes and provide help with defence planning based on Boer War lessons.

The dockyards were turned over at the same time, to be managed by the Department of Marine and Fisheries, and with a continuing obligation to support the Royal Navy when its ships visited the port.

An increasingly nationalistic population broadly supported the transfer of the bases, but the associated financial support was not forthcoming. As Roger Sarty has noted, a Canada busy populating the prairies "regarded this sudden responsibility with vast distaste." In 1907 defence expenditures did nearly double as Canada assumed its new responsibilities, but they always fell well short of the real needs as the international situation continued to deteriorate.

A few old documents located in the records of the 1st Field Regiment and the Princess Louise Fusiliers of Halifax yield interesting insights into the activities and problems facing the militia in the immediate prewar years. Always plagued by insufficient funding, units established a regimental fund administered by the officers, acting much like a board of directors. Its resources were used to fund such extras as a band, rifle team, and various sports activities, all very necessary to maintain morale. Its revenues came in large part from officers donating all or part of their pay; those of the 1st Militia Garrison Artillery in Halifax voted to continue this practice as late as 1914, when they were on full-time service in the forts.

Under militia orders each unit had to call a meeting of officers every January to review and approve the financial transaction of the fund. Sometimes the commanding officer also chose to comment on the professional performance of the regiment in the past year. In both 1910 and 1911 Lieutenant-Colonel Flowers of the artillery had to report that the past year had been disappointing, but hoped that the acquisition of new 6- and 12-pounder guns for training would bode well for the future. His successor in command discontinued such reports.

Some items for discussion arose so frequently that they almost became standard. Officers were continually being urged to give the unit rifle team more support, to make more use of the mess, and, somewhat paradoxically, to pay their mess bills on time. More seriously, the 1st Garrison Artillery had to resort to the regimental fund to hire a recruit instructor-cum-janitor at a wage of twelve dollars per week.

A former commanding officer of the Fusiliers had donated the Vidito Shield, named after him, for annual completion between officer teams from all units. Rivalry was fierce. Targets were set up on McNabs Island at ranges of three hundred, five hundred, and six hundred yards, and competitors were allowed to use a rifle and sights of their choice. In the years before the war the Royal Canadian Engineers and the Canadian Garrison Artillery were both winners, and on one memorable occasion the officers of *Niobe* triumphed over all their army counterparts.

In one regiment at least, new officers were recruited by a process very reminiscent of a private club. An interested person made an application, reviewed in the first instance by the majors commanding the four companies of the regiment. Their recommendation was passed to the commanding officer. Subject to his approval, a meeting of all officers was convened, each one having an equal vote for or against acceptance. If one in five ballots was black the applicant was refused without explanation. If accepted, he was enrolled as a provisional lieutenant, and his service indoctrination began. Under this system the officer cadre would continue to replicate itself in its own image, for better or for worse.

Halifax was largely bypassed by the wave of immigrants rolling west. For fifty years Nova Scotia's prosperity had depended on the building and sailing of wooden vessels. But the advent of steam propulsion and iron ships spelled the end of the golden age, foreshadowed when, during the American Civil War, the British fleet in Halifax consisted entirely of steamers. Capital and industry fled the city as the shipbuilding industry withered. In *Halifax, Warden of the North*, Thomas Raddall laments that "Halifax went into a unhappy trance for forty years." One of the few economic positives was the decades-long upgrading of the fortress, driven by the rapid evolution of military technology. Also, a dry dock was constructed just north of the dockyard, more evidence that supporting the garrison and navy was the only reliable industry.

Beginning in 1901 conditions began to improve. A commercial revival was stimulated by sales of Annapolis Valley apples to Britain, a significant increase in the value of the fishery, and the establishment of the steel industry at Sydney.

Although most were merely transients, the immigrant trade had a positive effect on the port, peaking in 1913 when ninety-six thousand new Canadians arrived in Halifax. As an ice-free harbour it was also becoming a seasonal export port for central Canadian manufacturers, foreshadowing its Great War role as the embarkation point for France. New deep-water wharves were constructed south of the existing piers, necessitating a railway cutting through the south end. In 1913 it was estimated that planned developments, both military and civilian, would generate total expenditures estimated at more than $51 million.

The 1911 census showed a total population of 46,619, representing an increase of 14 per cent since 1901. Overwhelmingly, the inhabitants were descendants of immigrants from the British Isles, predominantly Scots and Irish. Accommodation had cooled the sometimes fierce rivalry between Catholics and Protestants that had troubled society in earlier years.

True to its past, even after the gold rush era ended Victoria continued to contend with repeated boom and bust cycles.

Optimism had been high when the likely route of the Canadian Pacific Railway was to Bute Inlet on the British Columbia coast, and thence via Nanaimo to a western terminus at Esquimalt. When instead Vancouver was chosen as the transcontinental terminus Victoria had to be content with a line from Nanaimo to Victoria, serving only Vancouver Island. With superior rail connections and a better harbour, Vancouver quickly outstripped the capital in economic activity and population, enjoying a real estate boom that hardly touched Victoria.

In 1903 Richard McBride became premier of the province. He had been among the strongest supporters of Confederation. Blessed with charm, good humour, and effervescent optimism he was the man for the moment. When he took power, the province was on the verge of bankruptcy but soon enjoyed a recovery as the forestry and fishing industries became more stable and larger firms began to expand production. McBride encouraged the building of new railroads in the interior, to the point of virtual mania.

Mining developed rapidly, especially base metals from the massive deposits near Trail in the interior. But from the standpoint of Victoria, what really mattered was the coal industry centred on Nanaimo, 110 kilometres to the north. James Dunsmuir was a Scottish entrepreneur who consolidated many of the smaller coal firms under his ownership and ruthlessly made them more productive. Some of his financing came from wealthy officers of the Royal Navy's Esquimalt squadron, who were keenly aware of the potential of coal as the navy transitioned from sail to steam. He purchased businesses and property in Victoria, most notably the vast estate of Hatley Park on the western shore of Esquimalt harbour, where he erected a mansion reminiscent of the castles of his native Scotland. His wealth made him enormously influential.

A new spirit of optimism was evident in the city as the

Garden party at Admiralty House, a centre of social life when the North American and West Indies squadron was operating from Halifax in the summer.

old mainland–island rivalry became a thing of the past. A provincial library was constructed, along with the beautiful and impressive new legislature building on the waterfront. By 1907 Victoria was thronged with British settlers and boom conditions prevailed in the real estate sector. Social life became very active, with theatres jammed to capacity on a nightly basis.

Immigration was a running sore in the political and social life of the province. Those of British origin were welcome, but there was great opposition to admitting those from China, Japan, and India. Racism was disguised as an economic concern. Offered work for lower wages — and with no legislation outlawing discrimination based on race, immigrants from Asia were blamed for taking jobs away from the European-origin population. The British Columbia legislature passed frequent laws to stem the influx, but such measures were disallowed by the federal government. Businessmen like Dunsmuir fought the provincial attempts to limit immigration; many saw his motives as arising from his desire for cheap labour. The Canadian government ultimately responded with a head tax on Chinese immigrants and other measures to limit immigration. The British alliance with Japan in 1902 did nothing to lessen resentment of immigrants from that country, and the Japanese government agreed to impose some "voluntary" limits on emigration to Canada.

In 1907 eight thousand Japanese, two thousand Sikhs, and fifteen hundred Chinese arrived at B.C. ports. Anti-Asian sentiment was widespread, and Asian neighbourhoods and businesses were attacked in Vancouver. A federal investigation led by William Lyon Mackenzie King, then a young civil servant, concluded that the Japanese government was deliberately failing to honour its restrictive agreements.

The census of 1911 found that Victoria's population had risen to 31,660, an increase of over 40 per cent since 1901, and about three-quarters that of Halifax. Like Halifax, the inhabitants were predominantly of British origin, but with a significant proportion of Asian origin; Victoria boasted the second-largest Chinatown in North America, after San Francisco's.

In a 1909 debate on the naval estimates, the First Lord of the Admiralty gave the British House of Commons an alarming report on the relative decline of the Royal Navy. It was more powerful than it had ever been, but its margin over Germany's navy was steadily decreasing. In Canada, the issue caused greater disturbance than any other imperial matter since the Boer War. On March 29 the Canadian Commons passed almost unanimously a resolution indicating the country's readiness to organize a naval service.

The other dominions had made similar statements, leading to a Colonial Conference in July. Canada was represented by Minister of Militia and Defence Frederick Borden and Minister of Marine and Fisheries L.P. Brodeur. Director of the Marine Service Rear-Admiral Kingsmill attended as technical advisor. Along with Australia, Canada declined to help directly with financing the Royal Navy, but agreed to acquire a navy of its own. Australia did so by purchasing ships from British yards, creating a nine-ship fleet unit including a battle cruiser.

On May 4, 1910, Liberal Prime Minister Sir Wilfrid Laurier's *Naval Service Act* instituting an independent Canadian naval

Rear-Admiral Sir Charles Kingsmill was chosen as the first Chief of the Canadian Naval Service in 1910.

service received royal assent, after a stormy passage through a parliament deeply divided on party lines.

Canada's approach was in marked contrast to that of Australia, in that it revolved around national construction of a much less capable force. Initially, the infant service consisted of the dockyards at Halifax and Esquimalt, two cruisers purchased from the Royal Navy, together with their crews, some to be transferred to the Royal Canadian Navy, the remainder lent until Canadians were trained. Very ambitiously, basic officer training was to be conducted at the Royal Naval College of Canada, using the same curriculum as its long-standing Royal Naval counterpart. Provision was made for regular establishments, a reserve, and a volunteer corps, all the men to be volunteers.

A suitable choice for commander was available, the Canadian-born Charles Kingsmill, already commanding the Marine Service. Born July 7, 1855, in Guelph, Canada West, he joined the Royal Navy as a cadet at the age of fourteen and thereafter advanced steadily in rank and responsibility. As a captain he commanded three different battleships, his last being His Majesty's

Niobe *in peacetime appearance. Probably newly painted for a ceremonial occasion.*

Ship *Dominion*, in which he made informal visits to numerous Canadian ports before retiring as a Rear-Admiral. This careful grooming raises the possibility that discrete preparations for a Canadian navy had been taking place well ahead of formal action.

The federal government had financed the construction of a dry dock at Esquimalt as one of the conditions of British Columbia entering Confederation. By an interesting coincidence, when Her Majesty's Ship *Cormorant* became the first Royal Naval warship to utilize the new dock in 1887, her second in command happened to be the then Lieutenant Kingsmill, Royal Navy. Surely nothing was further from his mind at the time than the idea that the country of his birth would one day have a navy of its own, and that he would command it.

Based on Admiralty recommendations the government chose two ships. In 1910 the first was purchased, His Majesty's Ship *Rainbow*, an *Apollo*-class light cruiser. She was to be based at Esquimalt with the dual role of training and fishery protection, an urgent task on the west coast. For the east coast the choice was an armoured cruiser of the *Diadem*-class, His Majesty's Ship *Niobe*. An 11,000-ton ship, *Niobe* had a complement of 750 men, as compared with the 3,400 tons and 273 men of *Rainbow*. On commissioning, *Niobe* was commanded by Commander W.B. Macdonald, a native of British Columbia. For legal reasons the ships bore the designation "His Majesty's Ship" rather than "His Majesty's Canadian Ship," until they entered Canadian territory at the three nautical mile limit.

Both ships underwent extensive refits before the turnover. These included significant improvements to habitability to meet Canadian requirements, including the most modern of galleys. British newspapers observed that the Royal Navy had no need for such luxuries, recruits being plentiful because of high unemployment. It was, however, hoped that in time British ships would be equipped to a similar standard.

Niobe sailed from Plymouth on October 10, 1910. Captain Macdonald had received the following instructions:

> *On arrival in Halifax you will consider yourself*
> *under the direction of the minister of Naval Service*
> *of Canada, but you will receive instructions from*
> *the Admiralty as to the manner in which the*
> *formal transfer of the* Niobe *is to be made.*

The new navy assumed concrete form with *Niobe*'s arrival. To the salute of Canadian Government Ship *Canada* she entered Halifax harbour on October 21, 1910, the 107th anniversary of the Battle of Trafalgar. At the Imperial Conference proposals for a Canadianized ensign and bilingual college examinations had been turned down: already the psychological identification of the future Royal Canadian Navy with the Royal Navy had been symbolized. Not until after the War would the difficult process of cultural disengagement begin.

With a main armament of sixteen 6-inch guns the anchored *Niobe* was an impressive sight, at least to the uninitiated. In

Visitors including Admiral Kingsmill aboard the Rainbow *immediately after her arrival in Esquimalt.*

truth, naval technology was advancing at such a pace that the thirteen-year old ship was already obsolescent. On November 7 the smaller and even more out of date His Majesty's Canadian Ship *Rainbow* arrived in Esquimalt. That date was no doubt planned to coincide with the official handover of the dockyard from the Royal Navy to the new navy.

Nationwide recruiting began immediately. Community postmasters were the recruiting officers, and the initial medical exam was conducted locally. Postmasters and doctors each received $2 for each recruit processed. Volunteers also presented themselves for enlistment at the gangways of *Niobe* and *Rainbow*.

A significant event occurred on January 11, 1911, when twenty-one sixteen- or seventeen-year-olds from across Canada assembled outside the former naval hospital at the north end of the Halifax dockyard. They were the successful candidates in a competition to select the second intake of officers for the infant Royal Canadian Navy. No doubt several of the cadets had witnessed *Niobe*'s arrival. Of the twenty-one, eight were from the Maritimes, including five from Halifax.

The first officer intake of six cadets had been selected without competition, had not passed through the Royal Naval College of Canada, and by 1911 were already undergoing training in Canadian Government Ship *Canada*.

Among the twenty-one cadets shivering on the college steps that day were five who will enter our story later. One, William Maitland-Dougall, was from British Columbia. Malcolm Cann was from Yarmouth, Nova Scotia, and John Hatheway from Fredericton. Arthur Silver and William Palmer were both from Halifax, Silver a son of a Halifax Rifles officer who served in the second Riel Rebellion, and Palmer the son of a Royal Engineer sergeant who had transferred in the same rank to the Royal Canadian Engineers when the fortress was turned over to the Dominion in 1906.

Australia had bought from Britain, but Canada's new navy was to be home-grown. The government requested tenders to build in Canada a fleet to consist of one *Boadicea*-class heavy cruiser, four smaller *Weymouth*-class cruisers and six destroyers. It was later decided to retain *Niobe* in lieu of the proposed heavy cruiser. Buying from established British yards would have been cheaper and quicker, but fostering a Canadian shipbuilding industry was desired on both economic and political grounds, considerations that have influenced military procurement ever since. The industrial capability had to be created, so the government promoted the establishment in Montreal of a subsidiary of the British firm of Vickers Ltd., to be known as Canadian Vickers.

The new navy seemed to have an exciting future. Unfortunately, it was nearly rendered stillborn by a legal issue that placed unacceptable constraints on its operations. The Admiralty law officers helpfully pointed out that, under Britain's *Colonial Laws Validity Act*, legislation passed by British colonies applied only within their territorial limits. Thus, it was argued that the *Naval Discipline Act* could not be enforced once Canadian ships sailed more than three miles from the coast. Accordingly, in December 1911 *Niobe*'s first scheduled cruise to Bermuda and the Caribbean had to be cancelled. She was to have carried Lord Grey, the Governor General, who remonstrated to the Colonial Office that a valuable opportunity to promote commercial ties

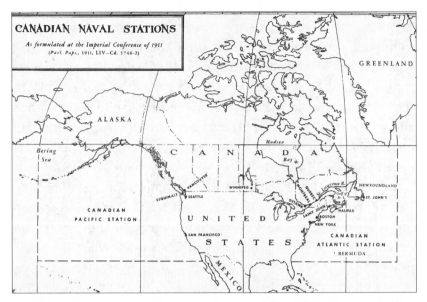

Royal Canadian Navy peacetime operating areas before WWI. Voyages outside this area required British permission.

with the area had been squandered. As the ships remained alongside training suffered severely, and men who had joined to see the world grew tired of Halifax and Esquimalt harbours. Morale suffered, and desertions increased.

Naturally, Canada vehemently protested. Minister Brodeur even stated that if he had known that the navy was to be confined within the three-mile limit he would never have supported its creation. The Canadian government's position was that its warships were by definition Canadian territory in which Canadian laws applied.

The dispute was not resolved in Canada's favour until the Imperial Conference of spring 1911. Agreement was also reached on the creation of a sector on each coast within which Canadian ships could operate in peacetime without prior Admiralty approval. On the Atlantic coast the area covered the area north of latitude 30° north and west of longitude 40° west. That same meridian was also the eastern boundary of the area of responsibility of the admiral commanding the Royal Navy's North America and West Indies Station. In the Pacific the equivalents were north of latitude 30° north and east of longitude 180°. In the event of war, the Canadian government could decide when and which ships would be placed under Admiralty direction, but once assigned the Royal Navy would retain complete operational control for the duration.

In April and May of 1911 *Niobe* made separate cruises to Saint John and Digby. On May 25 she left for Quebec carrying the Royal Canadian Navy's contingent to the coronation of King George V. She then visited Charlottetown, where rifle practice was carried out in Hillsborough Bay, before steaming via Richibucto to Quebec to re-embark the coronation contingent for Halifax.

Admiral Kingsmill had wished to continue the training program, but was unable to resist pressure for the ship to make a visit to Yarmouth, Nova Scotia, to enhance the political interests of the local member of parliament. *Niobe* therefore proceeded to Yarmouth, and spent five days participating in the local festivities. Because of adverse weather the visit was not a success from a political or any other standpoint. On leave at his family home, Cadet Malcolm Cann seized the chance to join the cruiser for the return voyage to Halifax. On July 29, 1911, she sailed for Shelburne to take part in Old Home Week.

Allowing for the anticipated tidal current, *Niobe*'s navigator laid-off a track passing to seaward of the outlying buoys and clearing the Southwest Ledge off Cape Sable by half a mile. The ship's position could be ascertained as each buoy was passed, as well as by the bearings of the various lighthouses. The navigator left the bridge at 10 p.m., leaving orders with the officer of the watch to call him when Cape Sable Lighthouse or the Southwest Ledge buoy was sighted, or at midnight if they had not been observed. The captain visited the bridge a few minutes later and before turning in warned the officer of the watch not to get to port of the track; that is, toward the land.

The night had been dark and clear, but at about midnight the ship was enveloped in fog. Unfortunately insufficient allowance had been made for an abnormally strong tidal stream. Subsequent analysis showed that *Niobe* was four and one-half miles north of her intended position when at twenty minutes after midnight she grounded on Southwest Ledge. The engines were immediately put to full speed astern, but without effect, and the ship continued to pound heavily for the next two hours. She then floated off, and the captain was gradually able to move her clear of danger although one propeller was useless and the rudder was missing. Meanwhile the crew fought the internal flooding and brought it under control, partly by stuffing all their hammocks into the rent in the ship's hull.

The ship was later taken in tow, arriving in Halifax on the evening of August 7, where she anchored prior to entering dry dock for repairs. She would not steam again for three years. At the subsequent court-martial the Royal Navy navigating officer was severely reprimanded and dismissed the ship, and the officer of the watch was reprimanded. The court took the opportunity to commend both the seamanship displayed by the commanding officer and the professional behaviour of the ship's company.

Niobe's ignominious return provided opponents of Laurier's policy with an opportunity to ridicule the whole idea of a Canadian navy. Even William Palmer's former classmates at the Halifax County Academy noted in their yearbook "William Archibald Palmer . . . left us at Christmas to join Ye Mariners of England at the Naval College, and we hear he is learning to steer the *Niobe* clear of rocks."

The expensive repairs took sixteen months, during which time recruiting and training virtually ceased and many of the men lent from the Royal Navy returned home. In 1911–12 a total of 350

HMCS Rainbow *arrival in Esquimalt.*

men were recruited. Nova Scotia led the way with 134 volunteers; among the other provinces Saskatchewan and Alberta brought up the rear with one recruit each. The new service was far from arousing nationwide interest.

On the west coast *Rainbow* remained seaworthy and carried out a useful function in support of the fisheries patrols. American vessels were illegally poaching within the three-mile limit on the west coast of Vancouver Island. Although prevented by her draft from entering many of the inlets *Niobe* was able to arrest one of the intruders and turn it over to the Fisheries Service for prosecution.

In April 1911 *Rainbow* was due for a refit. It seemed unlikely that the government would pay a civilian yard to do the work, but Canada had ceased to operate Esquimalt dockyard after the turnover from the Royal Navy; the repair facilities had been mothballed and the civilian tradesmen let go. Fortunately the workshops and tools were found to be in fairly good condition. The *Rainbow*'s engineer commander determined to carry out the refit using the ship's own artificers, and within a few days the different shops were in full operation. Lured by the promise of free tobacco, volunteers from the Victoria jail provided the unskilled

Staff and cadets of the first entry to the Royal Naval College of Canada, January 1911. Five graduates of this class of twenty-one were killed in WWI.

labour to manhandle equipment to and from the ship and the shops, there being no cranes, horses, or trucks.

By June the ship was operational once again. This may have been the first but was far from the last occasion when Canada's resource-starved navy somehow found a way to do its job, thanks to the spirit and ingenuity of its personnel. Perhaps shamed by the example, the government gradually revived the dockyard, and it would be in full operation in 1914.

In the same month Commander Walter Hose, Royal Navy (later Royal Canadian Navy), assumed command of *Rainbow.* Concurrently, he held the position of Officer-in-Charge, Esquimalt Dockyard, and thus Senior Naval Officer, responsible for all naval affairs on the west coast.

Rainbow continued to conduct under-way training, albeit for a ship's company well below strength, so much so that she remained immobilized at Esquimalt for considerable periods. She visited Prince Rupert and other ports, helping to keep the idea of a navy before the public eye. On a trip to Barkley Sound she grounded briefly, but fortunately no damage was sustained. With *Niobe* still under repair, news that the navy's only other

Sir Wilfrid Laurier and Sir Robert Borden, successive prime ministers before WWI. Their differences over naval policy left Canada's coasts virtually defenceless in 1914.

ship was in the same situation would have further eroded public support, with unforeseeable consequences.

From 1910 to 1913 the annual number of cadets entering the Royal Naval College at Halifax declined from twenty-eight to four, and the total number of men actually serving in the Royal Canadian Navy fell from 704 to 330. The once-promising new service was withering away.

Nevertheless, some training did continue, including gunnery training in Britain for selected officers and petty officers. On April 30, 1912, the cable ship SS *Mackay-Bennet* entered Halifax carrying the bodies of 190 victims of the *Titanic* disaster. She tied up near the dockyard and *Niobe*'s sailors assisted in the melancholy task of landing the remains. Later, a party attended the memorial service and funeral.

With the encouragement of Premier McBride an unofficial company of part-time volunteers was recruited in Victoria in July 1913. In the early days training was provided by *Rainbow* personnel. In July 1914 the west-coast initiative was expanded across the country, ultimately being given the name Royal Canadian Navy Volunteer Reserve (RCNVR). In an emergency the navy could also count on the Royal Navy Reserve and Royal Canadian Navy Reserve. These were experienced personnel of the merchant marine, given some naval training and indoctrination, and capable of playing important auxiliary roles. In addition, a number of retired Royal Navy officers and men had immigrated to Canada, and might be available.

In the general election of September 1911 Laurier's government was defeated by the Conservatives under Robert Borden. The major campaign issue was Laurier's intention to negotiate free trade with the United States, but widespread opposition to his naval policy also played a role.

With Laurier's defeat, John Hazen, a former premier of New Brunswick, became minister of marine and fisheries. Kingsmill continued as Chief of the Naval Service.

As a convinced imperialist, incoming Prime Minister Borden believed that the country's security depended on making a direct contribution to the Royal Navy. In exchange, he hoped that Canada would have a voice in determining the foreign and defence policy of the British Empire.

His views were strongly influenced by his close relationship with Winston Churchill, who became First Lord of the Admiralty in 1910. British Columbia remained fearful of Japan, not withstanding the 1902 alliance, and therefore strongly supportive of naval development. As a friend of both Borden and Churchill, Premier McBride became a go-between in the crystallization of Borden's imperialist naval policy. In 1912 he received a knighthood, becoming Sir Richard McBride.

To maintain an acceptable margin, Winston Churchill considered that the British needed to build at an average rate of four and one-half battleships per year. Any contribution that an increasingly prosperous Canada could make to this enormous effort was critical. In August a secret memorandum from Churchill to Borden requested Canada to finance three of the latest class of battleships, additional to the planned British program.

Although tenders had already been submitted, Borden did not award the contracts to implement Laurier's policy. Instead, on December 12, 1912, he introduced his Naval Aid Bill in the Commons, providing for the funding by Canada of the battleships *Acadia*, *Quebec*, and *Ontario*, at a total cost of $35 million. Built in Britain, the ships would be transferred to Canada after sufficient Canadians had been trained.

Now heading the parliamentary opposition, Laurier remained committed to the idea of a small Canadian navy, to be built in Canada without delay. In the Commons his Liberals vehemently fought the Naval Aid Bill. Eventually it was rammed through under threat of closure, only to be defeated two weeks later by the Liberal majority in the Senate. Borden could reverse the situation by appointing Conservative senators as vacancies arose, but until then the bill was in limbo, and no funds could be made available to the Royal Navy.

These developments were carefully noted by others. When Borden first introduced the Naval Aid Bill in the House of Commons the German naval attaché in London reported:

> *It must be assumed that Mr. Borden's bill to*
> *place three warships of the newest and largest type*
> *at the disposal of the Motherland will be passed*
> *in the Canadian Parliament . . . It will now have*
> *to be reckoned that the three Canadian ships . . .*
> *are a net addition to the* [British] *programme of*
> *construction that was announced in March.*

Two weeks later he had better news for Admiral Tirpitz:

HMCS Niobe *in dry dock after grounding on Southwest Ledge on Nova Scotia's south shore.*

. . . the British Admiralty has been deprived indefinitely of the windfall of three battleships that they had hoped for.

Faced with the reality that neither Laurier's or Borden's navies were in existence, the naval service prepared a discussion paper on the Naval Defence of the Atlantic Coast. It concluded that eastern Canada and the separate Dominion of Newfoundland would become involved in any European war. In that event, there would be a threat from enemy raiders lurking in the sea lanes off Halifax. Moreover, the undefended ports of Sydney and Saint John might be raided for coal supplies. The paper recommended that the threats should be met by a floating defence, based in Halifax.

Admiral Kingsmill forwarded the report to the Admiralty. Now that the battleship idea was effectively dead there was little choice but to accept its conclusions. In the circumstances, the Admiralty recommended that Canada build a force of cruisers armed with 6-inch guns, both for coastal defence and to assist the

Royal Navy in trade protection. Essentially, this course of action would have been a reversion to something like Laurier's original plan. The suggestion was passed to Prime Minister Borden. He had little time to study it before the outbreak of war, when new priorities brought an end to plans for major warships.

***

The Pacific coast staff paper followed a Committee of Imperial Defence report of 1908. Asked to make an assessment of the likely scale of attack on the west coast, it was judged that an American assault was a very remote eventuality, and in any case likely to be made by land rather than by sea. The only perceived threat was a raid by two Japanese armoured cruisers, perhaps including a landing at Nanaimo or Prince Rupert to seize coal supplies. It recommended that 6-inch batteries should be installed at Prince Rupert and Vancouver, but the plan was not implemented before the war. In October 1912 an Admiralty memo recognized the strategic value of Esquimalt as a coaling station and subsidiary naval base, with defences able to resist an attack by unarmoured cruisers. Arguably, the existing batteries met that requirement; in any case no additions were made.

Interestingly, the threat of the powerful China-based Far East squadron of the German navy was not mentioned; this was the threat that would actually materialize in 1914.

If the navy was in disarray, the army could claim that its ability to defend the two coastal fortresses had markedly improved. We have seen that, beginning in 1903, strong measures had been taken to improve militia organization and training, and that the strength of the permanent force had been increased. The country had been divided into military districts with devolved responsibility for administration and training of the regular and militia units in their area, including Military District 6 in Halifax and Military

District 11 at Victoria. To foster the development of higher level formations the eastern military districts were designated divisions in 1910, Military District 6 becoming the 6th Division.

Perhaps most importantly, emergency planning had taken on a new urgency and sophistication. Early in the century Britain had begun to develop a plan covering not only the armed forces but every department of government, known as the War Book. In the event of a dangerous rise in international tension these precautionary measures were to be phased in, so that if war did break out the country would not be caught unprepared. The phasing-in was an extremely delicate process. It was vitally important to be as ready as possible if the worst actually happened. But it was equally important to avoid creating undue alarm in the population or provoking a premature hostile reaction from potential enemies.

The dominions were asked to follow the British example and produce their own War Books. In Canada, the joint committee of the militia and the naval service had begun to work on the problem in 1911, but it was not until early January 1914 that the government was persuaded to set up a full interdepartmental committee that included the deputy ministers of other government departments. That committee was actually meeting on July 29 when the warning telegram signifying war was received, but fortunately its work was all but complete.

Part of the overall plan was the drafting of port defence schemes for both Halifax and Esquimalt. Traditional doctrine had stipulated that ships were not to be tied to the defence of their supporting bases. The navy's tasks had been limited to blocking inessential channels and establishing an examination service to vet merchant vessels before allowing them to enter the harbour proper. It was increasingly recognized that destroyers and submarines had become key weapons in repelling attacks by cruiser raiders and torpedo boats, and their participation had to be integrated with that of the army. Unfortunately, in 1914 the Royal Canadian Navy had few resources to integrate. The defence schemes will be more fully described in the following chapter.

The 6th Division, with headquarters at Halifax, included all the Maritime provinces. The regular units in the Halifax garrison included the battalion of the Royal Canadian Regiment of Infantry at Wellington Barracks, just below which a large bombproof magazine had been constructed. The 1st Company of regular-force garrison artillery had custody of the batteries, and formed the expert nucleus of troops that would man the different forts on mobilization. Apart from local responsibilities, Halifax was the national training school for the entire garrison artillery, and being the experts in large-calibre gunnery, also trained the heavy and siege batteries of the mobile component of the Royal Canadian Artillery.

Royal Canadian Engineers maintained the fabric of the forts, barracks, and other installations and played a vital role as operators of the searchlight system and providers of electrical and other services for the works and their defenders. Both these regular units were still partly made up of ex-British soldiers, such as Sergeant Palmer, who had chosen to transfer to the Canadian army when the imperial garrison was withdrawn. Many may have regretted their decision, for under Canadian control funding for equipment and training was quite inadequate in most years leading up to the war. But had the pool of expert transferees not existed, the decay of the fortresses and their garrisons might have become irreversible.

In an emergency the regular nucleus would be reinforced in the first instance by local militia, including two battalions of infantry. The regular garrison artillery was backed up by the 1st militia regiment of garrison artillery; at the outbreak of war the regular engineers had no militia counterpart. Units from elsewhere in 6th Division would also join the garrison to provide

Cartoon referring to British Columbia's immigration issue. While European immigrants were welcome in British Columbia, those from Asia were not.

a mobile force for landward defence.

Regular and militia units in British Columbia were grouped in Military District 11, headquartered at Work Point Barracks in Esquimalt. On the final departure of the British garrison in 1906 the Esquimalt fortifications had been garrisoned by the 5th Company of Canadian regular garrison artillery and regular-force engineers, again both partly composed of British troops who had transferred. Because of desertions and ineffective leadership not enough men remained to train themselves properly, let alone train the militia. In August 1911 the Chief of General Staff, Major-General Colin Mackenzie, went so far as to recommend that the garrison be relocated to Halifax, where they could train and be sent back by rail in an emergency.

Sam Hughes had become minister of militia in the Borden government and insisted that the garrison stay at Esquimalt. He also decreed that the 9.2-inch rifled muzzle-loaders left in pieces on Signal Hill for the last ten years should be mounted and the position cleaned up. This decision may have been triggered by the suggestion that one of the two big guns should be transferred east to bolster the Halifax defences. Since no fire control system was installed, at least initially, the Signal Hill battery was of minimal fighting value; Hughes's decision was almost purely political.

The economic situation in British Columbia rapidly deteriorated as the railway boom came to an end in 1913. There was
serious unemployment throughout the province. The Victoria
real estate market crashed. Widespread and prolonged strikes
occurred in the Nanaimo coal mines, the strikers being financed
by a large American trades union. In August riots broke out,
with looting and destruction of property, as strikers confronted
strike-breakers, some of whom were Asian immigrants. To
preserve order, fifty regular gunners of 5th Company garrison
artillery, plus seven hundred men of the 5th Regiment and some
mainland militia units were rushed to the scene. Many militiamen thought the strikers had some legitimate complaints, but
they did not condone the breakdown of law and order.

There were serious injuries, but no deaths, thanks in large
part to the firm but sensitive behaviour of the troops, some
of whom would remain on active duty in Nanaimo for nearly
a year. They were in fact peacekeepers, although no one
called them that, unknowingly inaugurating a future Canadian
military speciality.

Commanding the 5th Regiment at this time was Lieutenant-
Colonel Arthur Currie. Knowing that the strikers were expecting
troops to arrive by train, commanders including Currie instead
sent most of the force by sea, thus establishing a presence without
risking bloodshed. A former schoolteacher, Currie had become a
realtor in Victoria during the real estate bubble. In difficulties after
the crash, he was alleged to have diverted his unit's mess funds
to his own use. He gave up his post in 1913 to take command of
the recently established 50th Gordon Highlanders militia infantry
unit, but the issue was not settled. Nevertheless, he continued to
enjoy the support of his friend Sam Hughes.

Many years earlier the far-seeing German statesman Count
Bismarck had warned, "The great European war will come out

Commander Hose aboard the Komagata Maru *during the tense standoff over illegal immigration.*

of some damned foolish thing in the Balkans." Throughout 1912 and 1913 Bulgaria, Turkey, Greece, and Serbia were at war, alliances forming, dissolving, and re-forming with bewildering frequency. Russia and Austria-Hungary were vitally concerned spectators. The year 1914 ushered in an uneasy calm. The Balkan Peninsula remained a powder-keg, but the two great powers had not been drawn in. As a result, according to Churchill, "Spring and summer . . . were marked in Europe by an exceptional tranquillity." Fittingly, during that period Europe enjoyed many months of exceptionally fine weather.

In the spring of 1914 *Rainbow* was involved in an unfortunate incident arising from British Columbia's historic opposition to Asian immigration. In May the Japanese merchant vessel *Komagata Maru* arrived in Vancouver with four hundred Sikhs who hoped to settle in Canada. Many were veterans of the British Indian Army, but it was alleged that a nationalist group had chartered the *Komagata* and that the immigrants would be a disruptive

Sikh immigrants aboard ship in Vancouver harbour, 1914. HMCS Rainbow
would force the Komagata Maru *to sail without disembarking the passengeers.*

influence. The Sikhs were not allowed to land and stayed in the
anchored ship for two months. In mid-July, 175 police attempted
to remove them, with the intention of shipping them home in the
CPR liner *Empress of India*. They were prevented from boarding
by volleys of coal from the ship's bunkers and retired in disorder.

Rainbow was in Esquimalt preparing for a patrol of the seal
fishery in the Bering Strait, her crew bolstered by a contingent lent from *Niobe*. Ordered to Vancouver, she arrived on
the morning of July 17. Obsolescent though she was, in this
confined scenario she created an impression of overwhelming
force that discouraged the immigrants. They agreed to leave,
after semaphoring the message, "Our only ammunition is
coal!" *Komagata Maru* was prepared for sea, and escorted out
of harbour and through the Strait of Juan de Fuca by *Rainbow*.
Commander Hose had done his duty, but no one could take
pride in what had occurred.

CHAPTER FOUR
Defences, Defenders, and the Coming of War, August 1914

On the eve of war Canada was far from ready, not least from a military standpoint. However, despite a chronic lack of financial support the last several years had seen considerable improvement. The militia council and the interdepartmental committee of the army and navy were valuable advisors to the responsible ministers. At 3,110 officers and men the permanent force was both larger and more professional than ever, and the active militia numbered seventy-four thousand, of course with varying levels of training. The War Book was in existence, as were defence schemes for the fortresses on both coasts. A new fort was being built at already well-defended Halifax, and Esquimalt remained as the focus of west-coast activity. Of course the navy was a mess, but only four years earlier the country had no navy at all.

The joint army–navy plans for the protection of the fortresses were embodied in two separate defence schemes. Based on assessment of the various threats, the schemes set out in great detail the deployment of troops to the forts and batteries, and to

East coast operational area, 1914–1915.

the infantry positions defending against landward incursions. They also prescribed the location and manning of the guard posts protecting vital points within the defended area against saboteurs. The few naval measures were coordinated with those of the army, and instructions were given that joint exercises were to be conducted annually. Aircraft could have been useful in a number of ways, but as yet the country did not possess an air force.

On both coasts the navy was given the least important role. Partly this was in accordance with the no longer fully accepted principle that the navy should be free to accomplish its blue-water tasks rather than being tied to the protection of its own base. But in Canada's case the navy's very limited capabilities precluded a significant operational contribution.

Its most urgent commitment was to manage the examination service. Inbound merchant ships were required to anchor for inspection of cargoes and crews in a designated area off each harbour. The inspecting officers were usually Royal Naval or Royal Canadian Naval Reserve merchant mariners now on active duty, working from small, unarmed examination vessels. This task was coordinated with examination batteries, more fully described below.

Distinct from the defence schemes, the War Book stipulated that naval intelligence centres would be established at Halifax and Esquimalt at the precautionary stage of mobilization. They were to collate information obtained from coastal wireless stations for use by the local naval intelligence officers, and for onward transmission to operational authorities and Naval Service Headquarters.

The more critical role, assigned to the army, revolved around the fixed defences of the fortress. In accordance with coastal artillery theory of the time, the different batteries had specific tasks and were armed accordingly.

By 1900 the modern threats to coastal fortresses had been fully analyzed and categorized as follows;

1. Attack by one or more battleships.
2. Attack by one or more cruisers.
3. Attack by blockers or boom-smashers.
4. Attack by torpedo craft.
5. Land raid.

Together, these threats generated the need for the fortress guns to undertake three roles.

The counter-bombardment role was to engage large enemy ships standing off at long range, to prevent them from shelling the defences and dockyards. Counter-bombardment batteries were armed with 9.2-inch rifled breech-loading guns, situated to command a wide field of fire.

Batteries of 6-inch or 4.7-inch breech-loading guns were assigned to what was called the close-in role, but actually covered the intermediate ranges between counter-bombardment and short-range

Firing fixed ammunition, these 4.7-inch guns were important in both the close-in and anti-torpedo craft roles at Halifax.

action. Typical targets would be attacking cruisers, blockships, or boom-smashers actually trying to penetrate the defences.

The short-range anti–torpedo boat mission was to protect the naval bases from submarines, destroyers and fast attack craft using speed, surprise, and perhaps darkness to rush the entrance. Batteries in this role were armed with 12-pounder or 4.7-inch guns, using fixed ammunition to lay down rapid fire against fast-moving targets. One 12-pounder battery would be the examination battery, in which one gun was loaded and on continuous full alert, prepared to stop any vessel trying to leave the examination anchorage without clearance. No merchant traffic was permitted after dark.

Thus coastal artillery had to be prepared to deal by day and by night with everything from long-range to very close-in attacks, and everything between. Some batteries therefore had to be sited as far to seaward as possible, others at intermediate points, and still others at the very threshold of the defended port. Moreover, the guns within each battery needed to be capable of engaging the type of threat they were intended to neutralize.

There was a high risk that attacks by fast attack craft would be launched under cover of darkness, rushing the defences before they could react. For this reason defence electric lights, commonly known as searchlights, were an essential part of a fortress, and were incorporated in some of the batteries. They could be used singly, as a concentrated beam for locating and tracking a specific target, or a cluster of them could be used together to

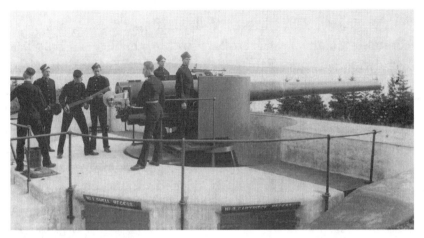

*6-inch breech-loading gun at Fort Ogilvie. Such weapons fired separately loaded
ammunition in the close-in defensive role.*

illuminate an area for the gun aimers. Each group of lights was
powered from a concealed and protected generating room.

At both Halifax and Esquimalt the close-in 12-pounder and
4.7-inch batteries covered overlapping arcs, able to plaster with
rapid fire the illuminated areas off Point Pleasant and Black
Rock, respectively. Acquiring and engaging very fast-moving
targets nevertheless required special equipment and techniques,
more fully explained in the Appendix.

All gun positions were expected to play a role in thwarting
attempted landings at locations reachable by their weapons. If
a lodgement was effected the works were vulnerable to attack
by enemy raiding parties approaching from the rear. They
were therefore protected against assaults from that direction by
trenches and concrete walls, loop-holed for rifles and machine
guns in the hands of the gunners stationed there.

In addition, a mobile force of infantry or garrison artillery,
equipped with 13-pounder field guns and Maxim machine
guns, would seek out and destroy the intruders before they
reached the forts.

The defence was directed and coordinated using a system common to all coastal artillery within the British Empire's worldwide network of fortresses. Overall control was exercised by commanders in fire command posts where staff plotted target information, and passed the grid location to specific batteries for engagement. The reader is referred to the Appendix for a more detailed description of the standard operational procedures.

Well-planned and reasonably well-equipped as these defences were, success would ultimately depend on the quality of the defenders by whom they were manned.

The regular artillery garrison was never large enough to operate all the batteries in war conditions. The reason was simple: in war, each position had to be manned continuously with rotating teams or watches. Much of the manpower required in a watch system would be superfluous under peacetime conditions, and was not provided. Each fortress or defended port therefore needed reinforcement from local sources to achieve full combat readiness.

***

The roles and composition of the regular-force garrison artillery and engineers have already been described. They were supported by detachments of regular service units.

The Canadian Ordnance Corps (COC) comprised technical specialists assisting the garrison artillery in the care and maintenance of weapons and ammunition, Number 1 Detachment at Halifax and Number 11 at Esquimalt. The remaining regular support elements consisted of detachments of the Canadian Army Pay Corps (Number 6 Halifax, Number 11 Esquimalt), Canadian Army Medical Corps (Number 4 Halifax, Number 9 Esquimalt), and Canadian Army Service Corps (Number 4 Halifax, Number 6 Esquimalt).

The regular infantry component of the Halifax garrison

Fort Rodd searchlight. Searchlights were essential in defending the ports at night against fast attack craft.

was the 1st Battalion, Royal Canadian Regiment, quartered in Wellington Barracks. Two of its companies were detached to London and Toronto.

The 1st and 5th Regiments of militia garrison artillery were the reinforcement units for the regulars on their respective coasts. In principle their members were capable of performing most of the same functions as their regular counterparts. Their training had been stinted in recent years, and being part-timers the men could not sustain the same combat capability as regulars, but the 5th Regiment at least was regarded as one of the most effective units in the entire militia.

The two militia infantry units in the Halifax garrison were the 63rd Regiment, Halifax Rifles, and the 66th Regiment, Princess Louise Fusiliers. Both are in existence today. The 63rd Regiment was first organized in 1860 as the Halifax Volunteer Battalion. It did garrison duty during the Fenian raids, and all 109 ranks served in the second Riel Rebellion. The 66th Regiment, Princess Louise Fusiliers, traces its history to Cornwallis's Halifax

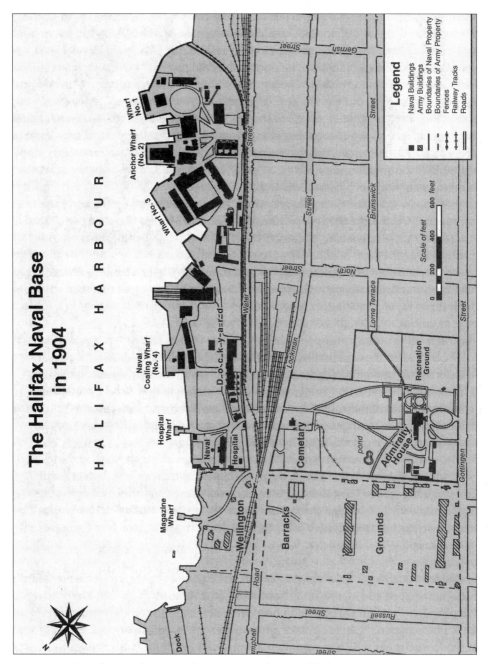

Largely neglected after 1906, the Base was substantially the same in 1914.

Battalion of 1749, renamed as the 63rd Regiment, Halifax Battalion of Volunteer Infantry, in 1867 and 1869. In the Riel Rebellion it contributed three companies to the Halifax provisional battalion and later sent more volunteers to the Boer War than any other militia unit. After an inspection by Governor General the Marquis of Lorne, accompanied by his consort Princess Louise, it received the name Princess Louise Fusiliers.

The local forces would be reinforced by three militia units from outside the Halifax area: the 62nd Infantry Regiment from Saint John, the cavalry of the 14th King's Canadian Hussars of Kentville, and the gunners of the 3rd New Brunswick Field Regiment, forming the field force to thwart attacks by land. Subsequent recruiting of all the militia units to their wartime establishments, an approximate doubling, would bring the garrison to its planned strength of approximately 6,700 officers and men.

There was no militia or regular infantry unit in Esquimalt. In case of landings, field protection for the forts and batteries was provided by the 3rd Company of the militia artillery, made up of men trained as infantry and provided with Maxim machine guns and 13-pounder muzzle-loading field guns. On mobilization they were to be reinforced by the 6th Regiment, Duke of Connaught's Own Rifles, a Vancouver unit.

After the 1906 transfer a colonel of the regular Canadian army commanded both the Maritime provinces' Military District 6 and the Halifax fortress, including the militia component of the garrison. He was always an artillery man. The first incumbent was Colonel C.W. Drury, but in 1914 the post was held by R.W. Rutherford, first as a colonel, and later as brigadier, and finally major-general. He had originally served in the Halifax militia, and joined the regular force in 1883. At Militia Headquarters from 1901, he helped plan the 1912 and 1914 major revisions to the fortress defence schemes. With this background he was

Replica of 9.2-inch gun barrel at Signal Hill. These huge weapons assumed the counter-bombardment role in the defences.

the ideal commander on the outbreak of war. Importantly, he enjoyed the confidence of the Chief of General Staff, Colonel Willoughby Gwatkin, key to the resolution of some serious issues that would arise.

The naval command situation at Halifax was clear. As Senior Naval Officer, Captain E.H. Martin, Royal Navy, commanded the shore establishments, including the dockyard and the Naval College. In peacetime *Niobe*'s captain responded to Naval Service Headquarters, but if his ship was placed under the operational control of the Admiralty he would come under the orders of the North America and West Indies Station, and would form part of the Royal Navy's 4th Cruiser Squadron.

Rutherford's opposite number in British Columbia's Military District 11 was Colonel Alexandre Roy. Without Rutherford's background or personal qualities Roy did not enjoy the full confidence of his staff or his superiors, and would be severely tested under the pressure of events. He was not the fortress commander, that position being held by the commanding officer of the regular-force garrison artillery.

Canadian Garrison Artillery engaged in field-gun drill at the Citadel. Mobile artillery was needed to defend fortresses against attack by land.

Naval command on the west coast was less satisfactory. Commander Walter Hose figuratively wore two hats, being commanding officer of *Rainbow* while simultaneously being Senior Naval Officer, the sole position Captain Martin held in Halifax. Although attractive to a cheese-paring government, the arrangement functioned badly when Hose was unavailable. When *Rainbow* sailed he perforce chose as a substitute one of *Rainbow*'s junior officers, who temporarily remained behind with all the Senior Naval Officer's authority, often unable to communicate with his superior. This was a recipe for trouble. The Royal Canadian Navy's first official historian has compared the situation to Gilbert and Sullivan's comic opera *H.M.S. Pinafore*.

***

As the German navy built larger and larger battleships it became necessary to widen the Kiel Canal, which allowed the

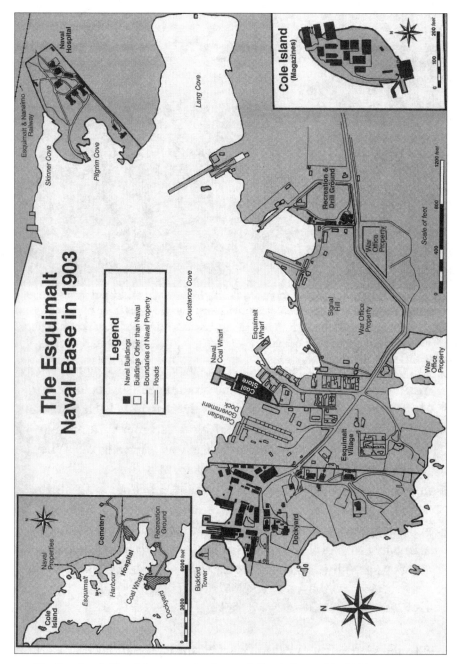

The Esquimalt Naval Base remained essentially unchanged in 1914.

fleet to pass between the Baltic and the North Sea without rounding the Danish peninsula. The work was begun at vast expense. The eccentric former First Sea Lord of the British Admiralty, Admiral of the Fleet John "Jacky" Fisher, predicted that its completion would signal that the outbreak of war was imminent. His words appeared to go unheeded.

In summer 1914 ships from several navies, including the British, were invited to participate in the ceremonies marking the canal's reopening. On June 29, in the midst of the festivities, news was received that the heir to the emperor of Austria-Hungary had been assassinated in Sarajevo, together with his wife. Exactly a week earlier, the people of Halifax had celebrated the city's 165th Natal Day in the usual joyous fashion, with horse and yacht racing, boxing matches, baseball games, and family gatherings everywhere.

Throughout Europe there was an immediate increase in tension. The German Kaiser cut short his annual yachting holiday and returned to Berlin. In Kiel the ceremonies and entertainments continued as planned, but there was a noticeable chill in the atmosphere. As the British squadron made its scheduled departure Vice-Admiral Sir George Warrender signalled to his hosts, "Friends now, and friends in the future," perhaps more as a hope than a prediction.

There was little doubt that the assassination was the work of Slav nationalists under the influence of Serbia, or that Austria-Hungary would seize the opportunity to settle with that country once and for all. Having been assured of German support, in late July the Austro-Hungarians dispatched a very severe ultimatum, but to general surprise the Serbians accepted almost all its terms. Amidst feverish diplomatic activity it seemed that the crisis might be averted before Russia felt obliged to come to the support of its fellow Slavs. But events were spinning out of control.

On July 14 the Royal Navy had carried out a long-scheduled test mobilization of its Third Fleet, normally maintained in reserve status. This was followed by the annual fleet exercises and ceremonial review. Normally the ships would then have dispersed to their bases, but on Churchill's direction the Grand Fleet was kept concentrated at Portland.

On the twenty-eighth Austria-Hungary declared war on Serbia, and Russia mobilized on the thirtieth. As alliance obligations were invoked one-by-one, the rush to general war proved unstoppable. Germany mobilized on the thirtieth, and on August 1 Germany declared war on Russia and invaded Belgium, triggering French entry into the spreading conflict.

The British cabinet was meeting twice daily. The official Warning Order had been issued on the twenty-ninth, triggering the phased implementation of the emergency plans. That night the twenty-four battleships of the Grand Fleet steamed darkened through the Dover Straits en route to their wartime anchorage at Scapa Flow. The next day the German High Seas Fleet with seventeen battleships transited the Kiel Canal from the Baltic. However, the German navy found little opportunity to challenge the British fleet during the course of the war except for occasional skirmishes and one potentially decisive battle.

The Warning Order reached Ottawa on July 29, setting in motion Canada's long-deliberated emergency plans. On August 1 recruiting was stepped up to prepare *Niobe* and *Rainbow* for operations, and personnel on leave were recalled. Midshipman William Palmer received the order while boating at Halifax's Waegwoltic Club, remarking to his female companion, "This means war"; by this stage not a particularly astute prediction, but a revealing reaction from a young man for whom war held an immediate prospect of danger. On the declaration of war, at midnight, August 4, *Niobe* and *Rainbow* were put at the service of the British Admiralty. The next day Minister of Militia Sam Hughes confirmed Canada's enthusiastic commitment with his announcement that a twenty-five thousand–man division would be sent overseas as soon as possible.

In 1910 the erudite Colonel Willoughby Gwatkin of the British army had been seconded to Ottawa to draft plans for an overseas contingent in the event of war with Germany. His concept called for detachments from different militia units to be concentrated at Petawawa, Ontario, for reorganization and training. Under his successor, Lieutenant-Colonel G.C.W. Gordon-Hall, the plan was significantly altered. The amended version envisaged the embodiment of militia units in their entirety, rather than through partial drafts, coordination being exercised by the various Divisions or Militia Districts.

Whatever its practical merits, this option fostered unit esprit de corps and morale, and was no doubt preferred by the militia. Sam Hughes was by this time the minister, and his well-known partiality to the reservists may have been a factor in the change. As a shortcut to reaching full strength at least one unit ordered 500 postcards in readiness to be sent to suitable individuals, asking them to state their readiness to do military service if called upon.

In July 1914 Hughes was still minister, and Colonel Gwatkin had become Chief of the Canadian General Staff. Forty-eight separate militia units volunteered their services, but under Hughes' direction the unit mobilization idea was scrapped in favour of the original concept of mobilization by details. Moreover, he ordered the first contingent of the Canadian Expeditionary Force to concentrate at Camp Valcartier, Quebec, rather than at Petawawa. With impressive energy Hughes planned and oversaw the construction of a vast complex of barracks and training facilities. Under his driving force the task was completed in time to handle the administration and training of the arriving militia, as they formed the composite units that would go to war.

Local units began to receive from Militia Headquarters a stream of telegrams providing detailed instructions on the make-up and itineraries of their respective drafts. Their own internal plans had become irrelevant. Reaction had to be improvised,

Sam Hughes, Minister of Militia in 1914, architect of a confused mobilization.

often resulting in great confusion. In many cases the regional headquarters were not copied on the pertinent telegrams, leaving them in the dark and unable to fulfil their coordinating role.

In succeeding chapters we will turn to the stories of the Halifax and Esquimalt defences as they responded to events. But it is important to keep in mind that they were doing so against the background of a confused general mobilization, as an unprepared and poorly armed country entered what would become the greatest struggle of its short existence.

On August 3, newspaper reports seemed to indicate that the British government was still hesitating over whether or not to go to war. In protest, Minister Hughes ordered the Union Jack flying over Militia Headquarters to be hauled down, but his staff soon convinced him to have it rehoisted.

The British ultimatum requiring Germany to respect Belgian neutrality expired unanswered at 12:00 p.m. London time, August 4. The Governor General had been vacationing in Banff, but had left for Ottawa on August first. In Ottawa, it was only 8:45 p.m. on the fourth when he received the telegram, "War has broken out with Germany." Canada was automatically at war also. Parliament was not in session, but most cabinet ministers quickly returned to the capital.

Since 1911 the minister of Marine and Fisheries in Borden's

British Fleet en route to its war station at Scapa Flow.

cabinet had been J.D. Hazen, formerly premier of New Brunswick. Political infighting had left the navy essentially impotent. The cabinet had no choice but to decide that Canada would make its main contribution on land, unknowingly exposing the maximum number of men to the catastrophic casualties of four years of trench warfare.

As the crisis unfolded official communications were routed between the Governor General in Ottawa and the Colonial Office in London. These authorities acted as central distribution points for traffic affecting all Canadian and British ministries. For speed and secrecy a special landline was run from Ottawa directly to Glace Bay, to be connected to the transatlantic cable. In operation by August 6, it was known as the Governor General's wire.

In accordance with the War Book, emergency measures were implemented to regulate finance, trade and commerce, and preserve good order throughout the country. The strengths of the Dominion Police and the Royal Northwest Mounted Police were substantially increased and the export of war material was prohibited.

Many recent immigrants to Canada had originated in countries that were now enemies, particularly ethnic minorities from Austria-Hungary, a nation that did not acknowledge any change of citizenship. A significant proportion of the immigrant males were still listed in the reserve forces of their original homelands.

On August 7 the government issued a proclamation for the protection of German and Austro-Hungarian aliens who continued to live their ordinary lives. It had earlier been suggested that the Department of Immigration should control the exit of reservists by examining passengers on boats and trains, but the suggestion was not followed through because of the alleged risk to Canadian–American relations. Accordingly, also on August 7, officers commanding divisions and military districts were instructed to arrest as prisoners of war all reservists trying to leave Canada. This power was extended to officers of the Dominion Police and the Royal Northwest Mounted Police on August 15. Aliens suspected of planning sabotage or espionage were also ordered to be detained, but could be paroled if they signed a declaration that they would not carry out any hostile acts and would report to the police at specified intervals.

German ships in Canadian harbours were of course impounded. Since Britain did not immediately declare war on Austria-Hungary, merchant ships from that country were given ten days' grace to leave Canadian waters.

Reports of strange aircraft flying near areas under military guard led to the first consideration of a military air force. In the meantime, flying within ten miles of thirty-nine wireless stations and eighteen cities was prohibited. Planes were permitted to enter Canada only across the United States boundary, and were directed to land as soon as possible at one of eleven airfields across the country. Before proceeding, clearance had to be obtained from officers commanding militia districts, and it was forbidden to carry explosives, firearms, Before the age of radio, and still less television, Canadians received their news entirely through the newspapers, which were instructed on their wartime obligations in an August 12 directive entitled "Memorandum on the Duties of the Press in War." These duties were far from unduly restrictive; routine reporting of ship and troop movements went on as though peacetime conditions continued to prevail.

The following general orders were issued for militia sentries across the country:

> *Militiamen employed in the protection of*
> *public works, buildings etc. will not hesitate to*
> *take effective measures to prevent the perpetration*
> *of malicious injury; and should sentries, piquets*
> *or patrols be obliged to use their weapons and*
> *open fire, their aim will be directed at and not (to*
> *the danger of peaceable citizens) over the heads of*
> *offending parties.*

A somewhat clumsy way of saying "If you have to shoot, shoot to kill."

On the brink of war the main threats would come from the sea. Coal was essential to the operation of both warships and merchant vessels. Quite apart from the danger of direct attack on the naval bases, on both coasts there were undefended ports from which supplies could be extorted by enemy warships under threat of bombardment. As we will see, modern ships of the German navy were active in both the Pacific and Atlantic oceans. In the Atlantic a number of swift German liners plied between Europe and New York. They were rumoured to conceal guns in their holds, and were partly manned by naval reservists. If and when armed, they would become a serious menace on the vital trade routes.

In 1911 a revolution had broken out in Mexico. Many

countries, notably Britain, the United States, Germany, and Japan sent warships to look after their interests on both coasts of the war-torn country. In 1913 the Royal Navy's east coast observation squadron had included Her Majesty's Ship *Berwick*, in which the first twenty graduates of Canada's Royal Naval College were undergoing their mandatory sea training as midshipmen. By 1914 the mids had moved on, but the revolution was still raging. The foreign ships on Mexican duty, including modern German light cruisers, were to become factors in the strategic situation.

Satellite observation and voice radio lay far in the future. Wireless telegraphy was still being perfected and was generally restricted to relatively short ranges. Most smaller merchant vessels were not yet equipped, and thus unable to report sightings until reaching a port with a British consul and access to the telegraph system. Long-distance telegraphic communication was by land or ocean cable, and far from instantaneous. It was therefore quite possible for individual warships or even considerable squadrons to drop out of sight for long periods. Rumour thrived in this climate of uncertainty, and erroneous reports would continually bedevil the operational picture on both coasts.

The danger from the sea was uppermost, but internal threats could not be entirely disregarded. Mention has already been made of recent immigrants from countries that were now enemies. Of course the vast majority were totally innocent of hostile intent, but, as the army's official historian states,

> *Conditions for the German secret service were*
> *extremely favourable. Crossing the boundary*
> *was practically unrestricted for citizens of either*
> *country. In the U.S. more than two and one*
> *half million residents had actually been born in*
> *Germany, and 40,000 in Canada. So there was*

*no section of the community in which a German
agent might not have been planted without
exciting the least suspicion. The German system
was controlled from New York by Captains Karl
Boy-Ed and Franz von Papen, naval and military
attaches respectively. In addition to planning
sabotage and carrying out espionage a main
objective was to bring the U.S. into the war on the
German side.*

On August 5 the Chief of the German General Staff urged the
foreign ministry:

*The feeling in America is friendly to Germany.
American public opinion is indignant at the
shameful way we have been treated. Every effort
must be made to take advantage of this feeling.
Important personages in the German colony [sic]
must be urged to influence the press still more
in our favour. Perhaps the United States can
be persuaded to undertake a naval war against
England, in return for which Canada beckons to
them as the prize of victory.*

CHAPTER FIVE
Halifax Crisis,
August 1914

On the outbreak of war the actual enemy threat in the western Atlantic consisted of two German light cruisers: *Karlsruhe* and *Dresden*. At the time *Karlsruhe* was the German vessel in the east-coast Mexican patrol, *Dresden* was her relief. They were intended to meet and exchange commanding officers, after which *Karlsruhe* would return to Germany. The rendezvous never took place, and for the moment both ships remained unlocated in the Caribbean, operating independently. Together or alone, they could prey on the hugely important trade routes from America to Europe, and either or both remained capable of raiding Halifax or extorting coal from undefended Sydney, Nova Scotia.

Her grounding damage had been repaired, but lack of funding had allowed *Niobe* to become little more than a poorly maintained and severely undermanned hulk. She could play no part in the conflict until these deficiencies had been made good and the ship recommisioned. An editorial in the Halifax *Herald* included the sentence: "When the mighty clash of empires takes place little

Emplaced at Fort McNab, this 10-inch gun was the only breech-loader of that calibre ever to be installed in Canada. In earlier times muzzle-loaders of the same size were common.

New Zealand will be in the front line with a battleship, but where will mighty Canada be?" However, ships of the Royal Navy's 4th Cruiser Squadron operating in the area depended for support on the Halifax naval base. For that reason the British continuously pressed the Canadian government to maintain and indeed improve the fortress defences and support facilities.

In the earliest days of the crisis events unfolded with such speed that no account can capture the reality of the situation. The newspapers crackled with bulletins; the Halifax *Chronicle* published its first-ever Sunday edition and copies were given away free on the streets.

On July 29 the Warning Order was relayed to Halifax. Its receipt triggered the precautionary stage of the Defence Scheme, characterized by the mobilization of the regular force. The detached companies of the Royal Canadian Regiment were recalled from Toronto and London, and the Halifax companies were ordered to cease their annual training at Aldershot and return to the city. Using vessels of the Marine and Fisheries Service under naval

One of the two steamers belonging to the Halifax Garrison ferrying troops to McNabs Island, 1914.

control, a detachment of the regiment was dispatched to Sydney to guard the transatlantic cable terminal, accompanied by a party of censors to vet the traffic for security purposes.

By chance, Number 2 Company of the militia garrison artillery was already at its war station, Sandwich Battery, where it had been undergoing training, including fire at targets towed by the garrison steamers *Alfreda* and *Armstrong*.

The reality of the international situation was captured in the *Morning Chronicle* headline: **Austria Starts War. Fate of Europe Depends on Action by Russia.**

The next day Russia, July 30, Russia declared war on Austria. The regular artillerymen were ordered to man the Halifax forts and batteries, and the engineers activated the harbour defence searchlights. The *Chronicle* headlined: **World's Peace in the Balance. Austrians Take Belgrade**, and on the thirty-first it reported: **Halifax Garrison is Mobilized to Defend Province. Germany Won't Remain Inactive Much Longer.**

On August 1 Naval Service Headquarters advised the Senior Naval Officer Halifax that *Niobe* might commission, and at the same time asked the Admiralty if the Royal Navy could provide the crew. The answer was a rather curt negative, but efforts to prepare *Niobe* for active service nevertheless began. At this time she had a crew of approximately 100 out of her designed complement of 740. Recruiting was stepped up, and regular navy personnel were recalled from leave.

At midnight the examination service was officially implemented, its anchorage established near the entrance channel off McNabs Island. The Halifax examination service was the only one serving the eastern Atlantic coast, thus handling all traffic whether destined for Halifax or not. Only preliminary inspection took place before a vessel was permitted to proceed to Bedford Basin for a more thorough search under armed guard. Militia Captains A.N. Jones, S.C. Oland, and George Brew were detailed for duty at the examination battery.

On August 2 the headlines read: **Germany Has Broken Peace. Declaration of War on Russia Yesterday and on France Today.** Financial crises erupted in both London and New York, where the stock exchange was forced to close. Germany invaded Belgium, and on the third the country's king appealed to France and Britain for assistance. The British Foreign Office warned the dominions and colonies to be alert for a German surprise attack in advance of any declaration of war. The transatlantic cables and the coastal wireless stations were taken over by militia and the navy, respectively. The navy later closed down most wireless stations and installed censors at the remainder.

∗∗∗

By this time reports of warships belonging to potential enemies were being received from many sources. In the absence of a clear intelligence picture each had to be taken seriously, even though most would later prove to have been false.

Royal Canadian Regiment regular battalion on parade. Detachments were dispatched to Sydney and Canso to protect cable installations. The regiment was later sent to Bermuda to relieve the British Garrison for service in France.

Dresden and *Karlsruhe* were reported off the east coast. From another source a message was received to the effect that two German cruisers had been sighted off Heart's Content, Newfoundland. Credence was added to this report when the Admiralty identified them as *Berlin* and *Panther*; in reality, neither of these ships was ever in the western Atlantic. A British merchant vessel reported that the liner *Kronprinz Wilhelm* was preparing to sail from New York, fully coaled, a report that turned out to be true. Until the intelligence fog cleared Naval Service Headquarters suspended sailings from the St. Lawrence River, and the vital North Atlantic trade route was badly interrupted.

The Sydney region had long been recognized as an economic and strategically important area. Its mines and steel works produced a large proportion of the total Canadian output. Of even more significance, it was a vital hub in the network of the British Empire's worldwide communications network. Indeed, according to a French navy authority, "Great Britain owes its influence in the world perhaps more to her cable communications than to her navy."

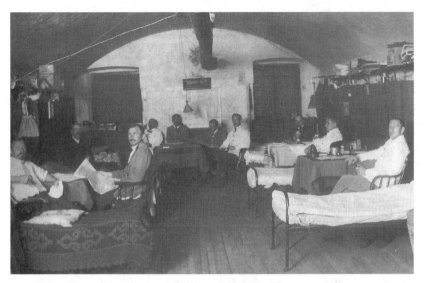

German prisoners in casemate cells in Halifax Citadel. Some of them may have been intercepted by Niobe *in the New York patrol.*

Transatlantic cables came ashore at North Sydney, Louisbourg, and Canso. After the 1912 *Titanic* disaster the use of wireless telegraphy expanded exponentially, and the Marconi Company constructed a very important receiving and transmitting station at Glace Bay, adding to the Sydney area's strategic importance. All these installations were vulnerable to bombardment from the sea, and to sabotage by landing parties or subversive elements in the population.

Several studies had recommended the construction of coastal artillery batteries to protect the area from roving enemy cruisers, but none had been constructed. The Royal Navy felt that the coast would best be defended by a force of 6-inch cruisers, but in August 1914 the Canadian navy had no operational ships on the east coast, and the four vessels of the Royal Navy's 4th Cruiser Squadron were grossly overextended in trying to protect trade in the vast area from South America to Newfoundland.

However, plans had been made to guard the vital facilities in an

In August 1914, reinforcements were rushed to Cape Breton to counter enemy threats. They included a party of sailors from HMCS Niobe, with two field guns as shown here.

emergency. There were two local militia units, infantry of the 85 per cent Gaelic-speaking 94th Regiment, Argyll Highlanders, and the 17th Battery of horse-drawn field (mobile) artillery. These would take time to mobilize. Therefore, the scheme provided that on receipt of the Warning Order two companies of the Royal Canadian Regiment would proceed from Halifax to set up temporary defences, one to Sydney–Glace Bay by train, and one to Canso by sea.

As noted, the situation was complicated by the presence in Canada of significant numbers of temporary workmen from Germany and Austria-Hungary. Both countries considered these men liable for military service in Europe in the event of war. During the Balkan crisis of 1912 many Austro-Hungarian reservists had been called to the colours and had left Sydney for the motherland. On July 29 the Austrian Consul General in Montreal announced that mobilization had not yet been ordered, but that if reserves were needed they would start at once for Europe. The total number of Austrian reservists in Canada was about ten thousand, including several hundred in the Sydney area. In addition, the numerous non-reservists could be called upon if necessary.

On August 4, the British government warned the Governor General that the enemy intended to begin hostilities with an attack on strategic communications at Sydney. At the same time the Marconi Company said that it had learned that several Austrian steam ships were meditating an attack on its Glace Bay station, and asked for immediate help. "In view of great importance of this station," the British requested that all possible protection should be provided.

In response a further detachment of regular infantry was sent from the Halifax garrison, adding to the temporary force already sent as part of the defence scheme. So threatening did the situation appear that on the night of August 4–5, an extemporized naval brigade of forty-three personnel from *Niobe* also set off for Sydney by special train, with two machine guns and two 12-pounder field guns. Among them was a no-doubt surprised Midshipman John Grant, graduate of the first Royal Naval College of Canada class, detailed from among the seven mids awaiting useful employment. A third special train followed, equipped as a hospital. Under naval control, the armed Fisheries Service vessel *Canada* also proceeded to the threatened point.

On the morning of August 5, a special train was dispatched from Sydney to collect rural companies of the 94th Regiment from Inverness, Baddeck, and elsewhere, and bring them to their war positions. On arrival at the Marconi station, some men were hoisted in baskets to the tops of the wireless towers to keep watch, a duty not likely to attract many volunteers. Four 4.7-inch guns of the Prince Edward Island Heavy Brigade were also sent, two to Sydney and two to Canso, and the militia gradually took over from the regulars.

It was either learned or remembered that *Rainbow* did not carry Lyddite ammunition for her main armament, nor was it available in the Esquimalt magazine. A special train was organized to transport the war outfit from Halifax stocks, but was

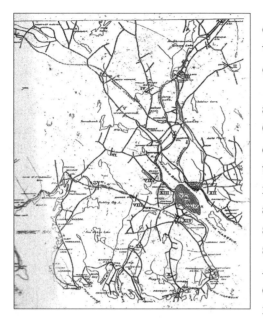

Halifax defence scheme, 1914. This was the plan followed by the garrison on mobilization, showing the location of infantry defensive positions.

delayed because the railway initially refused to carry explosives.

Reacting to the overall situation, Colonel Gwatkin authorized commanders of military districts to embody militia volunteers if absolutely necessary; seemingly, economy was still the order of the day. After consulting with dockyard officials, Colonel Rutherford called out one company from each of the Halifax Rifles and Princess Louise Fusiliers.

August 4 was the day of decision. Germany having rejected its ultimatum to withdraw from Belgium, the British government declared war, effective midnight Berlin time, 7:00 p.m. in Halifax. With Canada at war one of the government's first acts was to place *Niobe* and *Rainbow* at the service of the Admiralty. Naval Service Headquarters advised both coasts, "War has broken out with Germany," and requested the customs service to report names of enemy merchant ships to be detained in Canadian ports. The declaration of war triggered the War Stage of the Defence Scheme, including among other provisions the mobilization of the active militia. On the morning of August 5 the *Chronicle* greeted the coming of war with the headline **Britain Called Kaiser's Bluff, Forcing Issue.**

***

The Princess Louise Fusiliers paraded at the Armouries; ". . . excitement ran high because it was felt by all ranks that this being one of the oldest units in the province the 66th Regiment would be among the first to see real service." In this hope most of its enthusiastic volunteers would be sadly disappointed. The 63rd Halifax Rifles was also ordered out on the fourth, paraded at full strength at the armouries on the fifth, and moved to Wellington Barracks on the seventh. Now mobilized, the two regiments began to move to their Defence Scheme positions. The 1st Regiment of militia garrison artillery would mobilize two days later to reinforce the regulars in the forts and batteries.

The role of the infantry units and the mobile artillery of the fortress was to guard against ground attack by setting up a defensive perimeter. Commando-style landings to silence the Fort McNab and Sandwich Batteries were considered possible at the south end of McNabs Island and at Herring Cove, and if successful would allow the enemy to push toward the city. A larger-scale landing was quite feasible at St. Margaret's Bay, enabling an enemy to lay siege to the fortress from the west. Somewhat less likely, enemy soldiers could be landed at Lawrencetown Beach to threaten the fortress from the Dartmouth side.

None of these threats could materialize as long as the navy retained command of the sea in the local area, but this was by no means guaranteed: the Royal Navy's over-stretched 4th Cruiser Squadron was the only force in the entire western Atlantic, including the Caribbean.

Inner and outer defence perimeters were established. As depicted, they did not represent a continuous line of trenches but rather a series of camps and field works sited on or near major roads, and often with considerable gaps between them.

These were of two types. Numbers XII, XIII and XIV designated concentration areas for large bodies of troops, otherwise referred to as "Camps," and located relatively close to the city.

Numbers I through XI were assigned to entrenched positions on main roads, on a larger irregular perimeter, some of them being many miles from the city. These would serve as strong points or pivots around which troops from the inner camps could manoeuvre to repel an attack. For the most part they were not close enough to each other to be mutually supporting, and direct lateral road communication between them was usually lacking.

Positions on the eastern or Dartmouth side of the harbour were assigned to the Halifax Rifles, which also stationed one company at Camperdown at the eastern entrance to the harbour channel. The area included entrenchments and guard posts on McNabs and Lawlor's Islands. Apart from Camperdown, positions on the western or Halifax side were allocated to the Princess Louise Fusiliers.

On mobilization an infantry battalion consisted of eight lettered companies, each of three officers and fifty-seven other ranks. As the Defence Scheme was implemented B Company of the Halifax Rifles was entrenching on McNabs Island and D Company was in York Redoubt, but later moved to Camperdown. C and F Companies dug and wired positions on McNabs Island, and E Company on Lawlor's Island.

G and H Companies moved to position XII, the eastern camp site, between Main Street and Portland Street, more or less along the line of Woodlawn Road in Dartmouth. Their principal role was to safeguard the city's water supply at Topsail and Lamont lakes. At the time the two principal routes were essentially rural roads running through forested country; the present suburban street network was nonexistent.

About two miles to the east of the camp site, they set up forward positions on the north–south ridge between the two roads. The first was at Yorck's farm on Main Street, occupying the high ground a short distance from the southern end of Lake Lamont, with a commanding view eastward along what is now Highway 7. The second was a fieldwork at Kuhn's Farm in Woodside, on the shore road to Eastern Passage, probably on or near the site of the Nova Scotia Community College. Working day and night, the men started digging trenches, placing barbed wire and constructing blockhouses and dugouts to block a potential enemy landing force.

Inner position XIII was immediately west of Halifax, running south from the junction of the Bedford and Kearney Lake Roads as far as the Chain Lakes near the head of the Northwest Arm. It dominated the St. Margaret's Bay Road as it approached the city's outskirts. At the time the Chain Lakes and Long Lake were the source of the Halifax water supply, a vital service always well-guarded against sabotage. The Chain Lakes Detachment made up of B, E, F, and G Companies and the machine gun section of the Princess Louise Fusiliers was posted here.

The last of the inner positions, Number XIV, was situated near Spryfield, around Long Lake and Williams Lake, and covering the critical junctions where Prospect Road, Sambro Road and Herring Cove–Ketch Harbour Roads diverge as they leave the city proper. At that time Herring Cove Road started at Spryfield and ran south. The section of the present Herring Cove Road between Spryfield and the Northwest Arm was then called Spryfield Road, a street name that no longer exists.

At the southeast corner of Prospect and St. Margaret's Bay Roads were a machine gun and trenches protected by barbed wire. One company guarded the dam at Long Lake, living in huts while their less-fortunate comrades at other locations were under canvas. Two blockhouses of logs backed with stone and earth were constructed; Number 1 on the east side of the junction of Spryfield and Herring Cove Roads, and Number 2 north of the junction of Spryfield and Sambro Roads. At Herring Cove was an entrenched and wired position with a 1-pounder rapid-fire gun.

The positions on the outer ring formed three rough groupings.

Moving clockwise from the south, there was first of all a group of three on the Chebucto Peninsula:

- Number XI at Portugese Cove, blocking the Ketch Road Harbour Road.
- Number X at Ragged Lake, blocking the Sambro Road.
- Number IX at Hatchett Lake, another blocking position, this one on the Prospect Road.

In 1914, as now, there was no east–west communication between these three roads as they meandered through the wilderness in a generally southerly direction. The defending entrenchments could not easily be outflanked by an enemy moving north, rendering an attack from the south very difficult.

A second rough grouping of three covered the St. Margaret's Bay and Hammonds Plains approaches:

Number VIII straddled the St. Margaret's Bay Road at Governor's Lake. Some six miles further west was an unnumbered outpost at Hubley Station.

Number VII was on Kearney Lake Road, at the south end of the lake, and Number VI was at Hammonds Plains.

The British–American relationship was much improved, but full implementation of the Halifax Defence Scheme was still based on the premise of withstanding an American attack until help arrived. Implicit in this was the confidence that the fortress would then be sufficiently strong to withstand an attack by any other country. Strategically, the possibility of an American offensive after a landing in the Bay of Fundy or overland through Maine and New Brunswick could not be disregarded. However, such an operation would take many weeks to mount, allowing time for a reorientation of the defence. Thus, the positions covering the roads leading to Halifax from the north were essentially early-warning outposts considerably farther from the city than those described above. If the mobile component of the full garrison was mobilized it would use these positions as pivot points around which to manoeuvre.

The last grouping included five such locations:

- Number V at Upper Sackville on today's Evangeline Trail.
- Number IV at Middle Beaver Bank on the road from Rawdon.
- Number III at the south end of Grand Lake, on what would become the airport road and Highway 102.
- Number II, just east of today's Stanfield International Airport, at the village of Goffs on the Old Guysborough Road, nearly twenty miles from Dartmouth.

There must have been a position numbered I, but it is not shown on the plan. If the clockwise progression did continue from Goffs, Number I might have been at Lake Echo or on the Lawrencetown Road.

It would seem that there were, in reality, two defence schemes in August 1914. Consistent with the very low probability of American action, the one actually implemented was much less far-reaching than the one called for in the basic plan. There is no evidence to show that the positions in the last of the above groups were occupied in 1914, and almost certainly they remained unmanned throughout the war. In the same vein, the rural regiments that were to form the mobile component of the planned garrison were not called upon. The limited number of troops in the 63rd and 66th Regiments were employed in the static protection of high-value installations and the most vulnerable lines of approach, using the appropriate positions from the basic plan.

Full implementation based on an American threat would

have called for a garrison of six thousand men. But General Rutherford was well aware that in the circumstances that was not a realistic requirement. It became his policy to limit the garrison to what was reasonable given the German threat, obviously leading to a much reduced manning level. Even as early as the July 29 Warning Order he was inquiring whether the full scheme should be carried out.

Sensational accounts of mobilization in the Halifax press led Colonel Gwatkin to caution Rutherford:

> *You appear to be adopting measures applicable to general war with the United States rather than to existing situation. You are best judge of local conditions and requirements but as you will have to be indemnified* [sic] *hereafter for action you have taken not governed by existing laws to be careful to carry the local government with you and not to alienate popular sympathy and support.*

Throughout the war Gwatkin's aim was to maximize the number of men available for overseas service. For this reason, he consistently resisted the allocation of forces to home defence beyond reasonable military requirements. He therefore raised no objection when in early September the British government requested that the Royal Canadian Regiment in Halifax should relieve the British garrison at Bermuda for service in France. In advising Rutherford officially he explained, "North Atlantic now comparatively safe, and you would be justified not in neglecting reasonable precautions but in easing off a little of the present strain." This was followed by a personal communication: "Of course you have to guard against the insidious use of dynamite etc; for in Halifax as elsewhere there are sure to be

Canadian Garrison Artillery Band at the Citadel, 1914.

German sympathizers ready to do mischief. But at the present juncture you are in very little danger of German cruisers and German landing parties."

Rutherford was in full agreement with Gwatkin's policy, but subject to local pressure from senior Royal Navy officers for whom defence of the fortress was all-important. Rutherford proposed that two more battalions of the Royal Canadian Regiment should be recruited, one to be added to the Halifax garrison, and the other for overseas service with the expeditionary force. When the idea came to the attention of Minister of Militia Sam Hughes the reaction was violent. His antipathy to the regular army was notorious; possibly he felt that their units should be broken up and the men distributed among those of the militia, who alone deserved the honour of overseas service.

Rutherford received a blast that disturbed him greatly, but on September 8 he persisted with an alternative proposal. Instead of augmenting the regular infantry he suggested the establishment of a composite battalion formed from single companies drawn from eight of the Maritime militia battalions not yet called out. His superior Colonel Gwatkin agreed to support the idea, but, knowing Hughes's sentiments, expected that he and Rutherford would "go down together," as he put it.

The incident reveals the rift that had opened between Gwatkin and Hughes, who was generally supportive of enhanced home defence, largely for political reasons. But in the end the composite battalion was approved. By September 10 it was part of the garrison, relieving details of the Halifax Rifles who had been performing guard post duty. From then until the end of the war it maintained posts at the Gun Wharf, the King's Wharf, the Engineers Lumber Yard, the station hospital, the dry dock, and Richmond pier, as well as at Forts Clarence and Ogilvie, and Point Pleasant battery. It also provided guards for German prisoners and suspicious aliens confined in the citadel and on Melville Island. Many of the prisoners were enemy reservists apprehended by ships of the New York blockade while attempting to return home in neutral vessels. Thomas Raddall writes that the composite men were often taunted by small boys with the rough rhyme, "Comp-o-zite, they won't fight." In fact, most of them were unfit for overseas service. Their duties were essential if not glamorous, and the taunts were quite undeserved.

With some difficulty Gwatkin eventually got Hughes's approval to reduce the garrison to the level attained during the Precautionary Period. Rutherford prepared to stand down half of the Rifles, the Fusiliers, and the Canadian Garrison Artillery, freeing the men for overseas service. Two of the inner forts were actually abandoned for a short time.

But at this point superior arguments were brought to bear by Rear-Admiral Sir Robert Phipps Hornby, Royal Navy, commanding the West Indies and North America station and the

4th Cruiser Squadron. He was of the opinion that attacks in force by torpedo craft were improbable, but that a rush by cruisers or armed merchant cruisers or even boats could be attempted, especially in the later stages of the war. Alarmed at the reductions, he appealed to the Admiralty, which lost no time in reminding Ottawa that ". . . Halifax is an essential base for British cruisers protecting trade to and from Canada and the reduction ordered effects the safety of the base considerably."

According to M.S. Hunt, the admiral privately threatened that if the run-down did take place he would withdraw his ships altogether, and mine the harbour to prevent its use by the enemy. However that may be, the reductions were promptly cancelled. In a personal letter Gwatkin counseled Rutherford, "There is no cause for alarm. But I quite agree [with the British] that the situation will change when German vessels break through the Grand Fleet — as some of them, in the course of time, are not unlikely to succeed in doing."

This incident again illustrates the principle that if a dispute arose over the level of protection that the army should provide for an important naval base, the navy would have the final word.

In September 1914 the total strength of the garrison was about 2,600 men, rising to 3,200 over the next few months, and stabilizing at that level for the rest of the war.

The basic functions of the different types of coastal artillery were described in Chapter Four. The specific capabilities, location, and tactical features of the Halifax defences are outlined for reference in the note at the end of this chapter.

Due to the post-1906 funding drought, much-needed improvements to the searchlight system had scarcely begun. Initially, only six were working, four at Ives Point and two at York Redoubt. For optimal coverage the latter had to be repositioned to Sandwich Point, while top priority was given to the installation of two new lights at Fort McNab, with a mid-August target date. Further work on three lights at Connaught plus a fifth at Ives Point was also undertaken, using American equipment since British production was fully committed.

The 1st Fortress Company of regular engineers was badly understrength even in relation to the current requirement, let alone the emerging need to man new equipment. Militia headquarters authorized an emergency thirty-man increase in complement, and established Number 10 militia Fortress Company specifically to operate the searchlights. The 1st militia Field Company of Engineers from Woodstock, New Brunswick, was also added to the garrison. The much-needed new counter-bombardment Connaught Battery had been planned for years, but not funded. Construction had now begun, but the new work would play no part in 1914.

The regular and militia garrison artillery were in the most difficult position. An unintended consequence of the chaotic mobilization plan was the effective creation of three very different armies in terms of pay and conditions of service. Single men in the militia and the expeditionary force received the same pay, but married men in the latter received extra allowances. Meanwhile, regular army soldiers, whether married or not, received a significantly lower rate of pay than the militia. Typically, Hughes's reaction to that problem was, "Do not think that any not at the front should have extra and special [sic] treatment." It would not be until January 1915 that permanent force privates and non-commissioned officers began to receive the same pay as the militia and the expeditionary force.

Differing terms of service were also an issue. Members of the expeditionary force were enrolled for the duration of the war plus six months. In 1914 it was generally supposed that the war would be a short one, so much so that many rushed to get to France before the chance to see action was lost. The permanent force and militia on the other hand had a period of service of three years, extendible in wartime to four at the discretion of the government. A further disincentive arose because the regular garrison artillery demanded a higher standard of discipline than did the militia and expeditionary force.

***

The cumulative result was that the strength of the Halifax regular artillery was steadily eroding through natural attrition. Not one man had joined since the beginning of the war, nor would any be likely to do so until the disincentives had been removed. It followed that although most regular garrison artillery men volunteered for overseas service none could be spared, a further and decisive deterrent to recruiting. In *Nova Scotia's Part in the Great War*, M.S. Hunt laments:

> *The possibility of attack by German ships at first kept up excitement, but as the war progressed this soon diminished, and the men looked down from the ramparts at transport after transport bearing troops overseas. These were trying days for men keen themselves to go, and it was difficult to make them believe, as they were constantly told, that their duty was here.*

The British minister of war, Field Marshal Lord Kitchener, had stated that, "The front is where a soldier is ordered to be," which was true at a certain level, but little comfort to those who were tied to home defence against their will. As Hunt puts it, "They all knew that should the war terminate before their getting over they would for the rest of their lives be compelled to explain that they were not permitted to go, and felt keenly how flat such an explanation would fall."

HMCS Tuna *was the former yacht* Tarantula, *purchased privately from its American owner by Mr. J.K.L. Ross, and sold to the Navy for one dollar. She was armed with a 3-pounder gun and two 14-inch torpedo tubes.*

The staff of Militia District 6 (6th Division) managed mobilization for the entire Maritimes. The initial call-out was three thousand from the whole of the district, of which 2,600 were from Nova Scotia and 1,500 from Halifax. Since the garrison took priority, Nova Scotia was underrepresented in the first overseas contingent, and thereafter men could be spared for overseas only when replaced for garrison duties by new recruits, which were virtually nonexistent for the reasons explained above.

The Halifax Rifles and the Princess Louise Fusiliers were similarly constrained regarding overseas service. To add insult to injury each of the infantry units was responsible for setting up a recruiting system to engage and equip overseas volunteers before dispatching them for France, a semi-mythical destination much wished for by the men of the garrison, but seemingly forever out of reach.

Admiral Robert Phipps Hornby was always ready to resist any reduction of the fortress defences, and indeed continued to press for their improvement. But he recognized that the navy

could and should make a vital contribution itself. The Royal
Canadian Navy had already taken up and converted *Petrel* and
Constance for minesweeping duties, an essentially passive role.
But shortage of personnel and suitable vessels meant that patrols
in the approaches were at best irregular, and it was even difficult to support the examination service. But the most important
requirement was an active port defence, based on submarines
and torpedo boats, a threat that could not be disregarded by any
attacker. The Royal Navy being fully committed elsewhere it
would be up to its Canadian counterpart to do whatever it could.

What it did was to accept the irregular services of the
wealthy sportsman J.K.L. Ross, scion of a Montreal family
whose wealth was based on the building of the Canadian Pacific
Railroad. He spent his fortune lavishly on yachts, automobiles,
and race horses, and generally lived the life of a typical playboy.
But appearances were deceptive. At the beginning of the war
he presented Prime Minister Borden with a $500,000 cheque,
"to be used for the preservation of Canada and the empire."
He was a captain in Montreal's Black Watch militia regiment,
but being found unfit for overseas service volunteered for the
Royal Canadian Naval Volunteer Reserve, and immediately
undertook a private mission, probably with the knowledge of
and secret encouragement of the naval service.

Proceeding to New York, he purchased the steam yacht
Tarantula from the millionaire businessman William K.
Vanderbilt. She had been built in Britain from a design similar
to that of the Royal Navy's torpedo boats. Propelled by three
steam turbines, among the earliest vessels to be so equipped, she
could reach a speed of twenty-five knots. Vanderbilt had used
her to commute to his downtown office, arousing great resentment whenever her wake damaged vessels moored alongside.
Having fitted her out, Ross brought her to Halifax, arriving on
September 10.

HMS Good Hope *in Halifax August, 1914. She would become the flagship of Rear-Admiral Sir Christopher Cradock. At the Battle of Coronel in November 1914, she was sunk with all hands, including four Canadian midshipmen.*

Under American law at the time, anyone who knowingly:

> *fits out and arms . . . or procures to be fitted out and armed, or knowingly is concerned in the fitting out or arming of any vessel of any foreign prince, or state, . . . to cruise or commit hostilities against the subjects, citizens, or property of any foreign prince, or state, with whom the United States are at peace, shall be fined not more than $10,000 and imprisoned for not more than three years.*

Matters were presumably arranged so that Vanderbilt either was ignorant of the reason for the purchase, or could plausibly claim ignorance. But Jack Ross was certainly guilty under the law. The Canadian authorities went to extraordinary lengths to conceal the transaction. On August 24 the deputy minister of the naval service addressed the following letter to Ross.

> *It has been reported to me that the appearance of your yacht the* Tarantula, *now in Halifax Harbour, is so much that of a torpedo boat and so unlike an ordinary yacht that her*

*appearance on the coast might cause anxiety to
shipping if she were allowed to cruise, and it is
also quite possible that if she approached a man
of war at night she would be fired upon. Taking
all the circumstances into consideration, it
appears to be necessary to instruct the naval
officer in charge at Halifax to intern the ship
for the present. It would further appear that
this vessel, from her high speed, would be of
service to the government, and the department
would be glad to hear from you on what terms
you would dispose of her.*

Ross sold her to the navy for one dollar. She was then armed
with a 3-pounder gun and two 14-inch torpedo tubes. He was
able to retain most of the crew, all of whom were enrolled in the
Voluntary Reserve with appropriate ranks. If their naval pay was
less than they had received from Vanderbilt, Ross made up the
difference out of his own pocket. He himself was given a lieutenant's commission in the Voluntary Reserve and took command
of *Tuna*, as she had been renamed to further conceal her origin
from the Americans. Henceforth, *Tuna* played an important role
in maintaining the standing early-warning patrol at the harbour
entrance, and proved very useful in the investigation of reports
of suspicious activity along the coast.

The navy issued regulations giving it control of all traffic in
the harbour, and authorizing it to screen departing vessels, with
the help of the customs service, and, if necessary, to detain them.
It also started the process of buoying the entrance channel, outside which unauthorized navigation was prohibited. At the time
sophisticated pressure and acoustic mines were far in the future.
All mines were of the moored variety, floating not far below the
surface, held in position by a wire attached to a block anchor.

Small vessels acted as sweepers. Being of shallow draft they could safely pass over mines set for deep-draft freighters. The mines were swept by towing a special cutting wire between two vessels, a procedure not unlike the deployment of fishing nets, in which their crews would be well-versed. When a mooring wire was cut the mine bobbed to the surface to be exploded by small-arms fire.

The military and naval preparations described above were virtually completed by August 12, eight days after mobilization. Ottawa was informed that the Defence Scheme had been implemented, the sole exception being the buoyage of the channel, still in progress.

On August 10 *Niobe* had reported, "Ready for an emergency excepting engines, armament and boilers. Three of these ready except for tests, seven well in hand. Armament dismantled, partly replaced by four 6-inch." A warship must be able to float, to move, and to fight. At this point *Niobe* did not possess either of the latter two capabilities. When fully combat capable her armament would be quite adequate to counter individual German light cruisers and armed merchant cruises, but their superiority in speed would prevent her from bringing them to action except by surprise, at night or in fog.

The hastily dispatched naval brigade was recalled from Cape Breton, the army now in sufficient strength to defend the cable and wireless facilities. The Sydney area defences consisted of nine militia infantry battalions, and four 4.7-inch field guns manned by the Prince Edward Island and New Brunswick militia heavy artillery. The supposedly dangerous enemy aliens had very largely remained quiet, although several were arrested for failing to register, and three for possessing rifle and explosives. No damage was ever caused, and their sentences were very lenient.

Captain Martin was ordered to rush all of *Niobe*'s 18-inch torpedoes to Esquimalt by special train to meet an unexpected requirement, of which more will be heard in the next chapter. The train left on August 9. A draft from *Niobe* had been sent west to help prepare *Rainbow* for a prewar commitment, but was now recalled.

As we shall see, after recalling its Pacific Squadron the Royal Navy continued to operate two ancient sloops on the west coast, *Shearwater* and *Algerine*. After an exciting return voyage from their Mexican patrol duties they were quickly paid off. Their crews were railed to Halifax by August 22 to help man *Niobe*, and the ex-captain of *Algerine*, Captain Robert Corbett, Royal Navy, became the cruiser's commanding officer. Work on boilers, cylinders, steering engines, electric communications, and telegraph shafting was proceeding at a feverish pace under her engineering officer, Lieutenant-Commander J.F. Bell, Royal Navy. Additional 6-inch guns to complete her armament were expected. A full outfit of stores requested from the Admiralty was due to arrive on August 20.

In the last days of the month the ship raised steam and docked for examination of her underwater fittings. She then proceeded to sea and carried out a successful full-power trial, reaching nineteen knots, just one knot less than at her acceptance trials sixteen years earlier. On September 2 Captain Corbett reported to Naval Service Headquarters: "Trial most satisfactory worked up to 104 revolutions, ammunition completed to full stowage. Coaling tonight; have reported myself to Fourth Cruiser Squadron; leave here tomorrow for St. John's in accordance with orders received from *Suffolk*."

Thanks to the ingenuity and diligence of all concerned a near-miraculous resurrection had been achieved; it only remained to bring her complement to its authorized level. The order from *Suffolk* meant an order from Rear-Admiral Sir Christopher Cradock, commanding the 4th Cruiser Squadron, to sail to St. John's and pick up one officer and 106 ratings from the Royal Newfoundland Naval Reserve, all volunteers. The knowledge that Canadian rates of pay were nearly double those of the Royal Navy may have been an incentive.

In addition to the Newfoundlanders, the ship's company now

HMS Monmouth, *part of Admiral Cradock's Squadron, and same class as 4th Squadron cruisers in North American and Caribbean waters.*

included 390 Canadians, regular, reserve, and volunteers, and 210 officers and men of the Royal Navy, the total of 707 approaching her authorized complement. Naturally there had been no possibility of matching the personnel available to the specific rank and trade specifications laid down in the official establishment, and most of the volunteers had little or no experience. There should now have been a work-up period to develop teamwork and efficiency, but in the circumstances that luxury was dispensed with. *Niobe* was deemed ready to perform her first wartime mission.

On her return from St. John's the ship encountered a merchant vessel not flying any flag. The suspicious ship was forced to stop with warning shots. She was boarded, and determined to be the British steamer *Beatrice*. The chastened captain was allowed to proceed after hoisting the ship's red ensign.

Niobe reached Halifax September 9. Here she rendezvoused with the troop transport SS *Canada*, which had embarked the regular troops of the Royal Canadian Regiment. Always alert to the threat of raiders, the two ships proceeded to Bermuda,

RMS Mauretania, *record-holding transatlantic liner. In August 1914 she was diverted to Halifax to avoid German raiders.*

arriving on the thirteenth without incident. The Canadian battalion landed to relieve the British Lincolnshire Regiment, then garrisoning the islands, but required for service in France. On the same day the Lincolnshires marched aboard the transport and the ships returned to Halifax. The Canadian battalion would remain in Bermuda until August of 1915, when it too was sent to France.

The 4th Cruiser Squadron consisted of the *County*-class cruisers *Suffolk, Essex, Lancaster,* and *Berwick.* All were protected cruisers, lightly armoured, and carrying fourteen 6-inch guns and eight 12-pounders. It was the western Atlantic trade protection force, and relied on the Halifax fortress and base for support. In his flagship *Suffolk* Rear-Admiral Cradock was already searching the Caribbean for *Karlsruhe* when on August 4 he received the order "Commence hostilities against Germany." On August 6 wireless interceptions led him to a night rendezvous between *Karlsruhe* and the liner *Kronprinz Wilhelm*. The navigating officer of *Karlsruhe* took command of the liner, now commissioned in the navy, bringing with him fifteen regular sailors. One machine gun and two 3.4-inch guns with 290 rounds of ammunition were also transferred from the cruiser before the enemy ships were forced to escape using their superior speed. Thereafter both continued to operate on the trade routes, lurking menaces that could not be ignored.

As for the other ships of the squadron, *Lancaster* was at Bermuda preparing to guard the southern trade route, *Berwick* in the Florida Strait and *Essex* on her way to patrol off New York. In a one-on-one action each would be superior to the light cruisers *Dresden* or *Karlsruhe*, but, as the encounter with the latter had confirmed, they lacked the speed to catch them.

In 1906 the Cunard Line had finished two new liners, the Royal Mail Ships *Mauretania* and *Lusitania*. When launched the 31,900-ton *Mauretania* was the largest movable object ever built. She was fitted to carry 2,165 passengers, including 535 in first class, together with a crew of 800. Construction was subsidized by the Admiralty to render them convertible to armed merchant cruisers. In an emergency 6-inch guns could be fitted in specially strengthened positions on the upper decks, and provision was made for ammunition and gun crews to be embarked. To obtain the designation Royal Mail Ship the government stipulated that they had to be capable of maintaining a sustained speed of 24.5 knots, or 45 kilometres per hour. At the time reciprocating engines were standard in steam vessels of all types, but reciprocating technology could not meet the requirement. Thus, the two liners were among the very first ships to be fitted with Parson's steam turbines, developing 68,000 shaft horsepower, and consuming 43.5 tons of coal per hour. In 1907 *Mauretania* made the fastest-ever westbound Atlantic crossing, a record she held for the next twenty-two years.

Now in the early days of August 1914 a drama affecting the lives of thousands of civilians was unfolding in the northwest Atlantic. As the international crisis deepened, Americans desperate to get out of Europe crowded liners departing from continental ports. When she sailed from Liverpool at 4:55 p.m. on August 1, bound for New York, *Mauretania* was carrying 235 extra passengers. Hundreds more would-be passengers were left on the dock.

On this voyage her captain poured on the speed, averaging six hundred miles a day until fog forced a reduction. On August 4 news that war had broken out was received. To avoid needless alarm Captain James Charles, Royal Naval Reserve, chose to keep the news to himself, but as a precaution portholes were darkened and lights dimmed. Off Sable Island at 11:30 p.m. on August 5 His Majesty's Ship *Essex* broadcast a general message to British shipping in the Sable Island area: "Change your course, full speed for Halifax." This was followed by a warning of the German raider *Dresden*. (Had *Mauretania* been intercepted the German captain would have faced a dilemma. Being unable to send her with a prize crew to a friendly port, as required by international law, he would have been obliged to sink her, hopefully after allowing passengers and crew to abandon ship.)

Halifax was 140 miles away. Despite the fog, full speed was again rung on, and a violent course alteration was made to the northwest, directly into the sea, during which the third-class accommodation on the shelter deck was nearly flooded. The darkened *Mauretania* raced for safety at twenty-eight knots, spray breaking over the bridge, as her boilers generated seventy thousand shaft horsepower, two thousand more than designed. (Her chief engineer later said, "We could have gotten another knot out of her.") Wireless silence was imposed, preventing the dispatch of passenger telegrams, thus adding to the passenger's stress caused by the course alteration. The stress would have been even greater had they not still been ignorant that war had actually broken out. First-class passengers gathered in the saloon and joined in singing

"God Save the King." Among them was a group supposed to be German citizens, but according to a ship's officer who was present, they "chipped in and sang enthusiastically with the others."

The New York–bound White Star liner *Cedric* had also picked up the warning; she and her 868 passengers also steamed at top speed for the safety of Halifax.

Mauretania anchored in Halifax harbour at 10:40 on the sixth, in bright sunshine. Large numbers of spectators crowded the waterfront to view the famous and beautiful ship. Later in the afternoon *Cedric* entered the port, escorted by *Essex*. The cruiser proceeded at once to the dockyard where she coaled for two hours before hastening to sea again. As she passed cheer after cheer arose from the shore and from the passengers and crews of the two liners. Some percipient spectators may have realized that the incident signalled the re-emergence of Halifax as the key to the Royal Navy's operations in the northwest Atlantic.

The captain of *Essex* had ordered *Mauretania* to remain in port for five days, while a search went on for guns with which to fit her out in her designed role as an armed merchant cruiser. Numerous craft, including the Dartmouth ferry, were employed in disembarking the passengers to the downtown immigration shed. From there they were taken to the old North Station on North Street, continuing to New York on special trains chartered by the Cunard line. The only exceptions were Germans and Austrians who had not taken out American citizenship. Twenty-three Germans were detained in the Halifax citadel. The British Empire was still at peace with Austria-Hungary, but passengers of that country continued to be watched.

The only 6-inch guns available were needed to rearm *Niobe*, so *Mauretania* sailed unarmed for Britain for her conversion. But this would not be the last time during the war that Halifax would see the famous vessel, albeit in a different guise.

On the ninth three German-chartered colliers were reported to have left New York, probably in support of *Karlsruhe* and *Dresden*, while a fourth was said to be off Cape Race. The lighthouse at lonely St. Paul Island in the Cabot Strait advised that a warship claiming to be British was loitering in the vicinity, but had asked that its position not be reported. This might have been *Essex*, but as a precaution Naval Service Headquarters ordered all shipping at Montreal, Quebec, and Sydney to be held until the uncertainty was resolved. The Admiralty rebuked the Canadian authorities for this precipitate action, saying it amounted to doing the enemy's work for him, and sailings were quickly resumed.

Cradock was ordered to shift his flag from *Suffolk* to the larger armoured cruiser *Good Hope*, which had sailed from Britain to the western Atlantic. Baffled in his attempt on *Karlsruhe*, he proceeded north for the rendezvous. En route he received intelligence that *Karlsruhe* was at Puerto Rico and *Dresden* off the mouth of the Amazon. While passing New York he so advised the British Consul General. This information was reported in the *New York Times*. Transtlantic trade soon began to flow at its normal volume. Cradock could have coaled at New York, but under neutrality laws doing so would have meant that he could not use an American port again for three months. Better to save the option for a real emergency.

Late on August 13 *Suffolk* arrived in Halifax and immediately coaled, with the assistance of men of the Halifax Rifles who worked enthusiastically at this filthy and back-breaking task. It is not clear whether *Good Hope* should already have arrived; in any case she was not there. Unable to wait, Cradock sailed at once, intending to rendezvous at sea for the turnover.

On the outbreak of war all Royal Canadian Navy personnel had been recalled from leave, midshipmen Malcolm Cann of Yarmouth; John Hatheway of Fredericton; and William Palmer, Arthur Silver, John Grant, G.C. Jones, and J.E.W. Oland, all of Halifax, reporting on board *Niobe*. Grant had gone to Sydney as part of the emergency naval brigade. Once they were aboard, they found little to do in a ship that almost from a standing start was struggling to become combat-ready. Thirsting for action, and with *Niobe* jetty-bound, all seven quickly volunteered to join *Suffolk*. They were officially appointed, and managed to get aboard just before she sailed; a classic "pier-head jump."

Their departure was headlined in the Halifax *Herald*: **Brave Halifax Lads Eager to Strike for Canada and the Empire**. Despite the bustle of mobilization, the reality of war had yet to hit home. The article noted, "Halifax will look forward to their visits to this port throughout the duration of the war," almost as though they were sailing on a pleasure cruise. A few months later such sentiments would be extinguished in the carnage of the trenches.

On Saturday August 15 *Good Hope* arrived, and, according to the *Herald*, sailed on the same day, only half-coaled, hastening to overtake *Suffolk* for the change of flag. An older vessel, *Good Hope* had been brought out of reserve and hurriedly prepared for her mission, and because of a clerical error was four short of her established complement of midshipmen. The shortfall was to be made up from the Canadian midshipmen on board *Suffolk*. Naturally all seven volunteered. Admiral Cradock personally asked for William Palmer, who had been first in his graduating class, and for Arthur Silver, who had been the senior cadet captain. The other two were chosen by lot. The names of Malcolm Cann and Victor Hatheway were drawn. Service in a larger and more powerful vessel, and a flagship at that, was a step up, and the three not selected would have been bitterly disappointed. But within six weeks their much-envied comrades would be dead.

In the few days they were aboard *Suffolk* a very busy Admiral Cradock could not have learned enough about the Canadians to make an informed selection. But the mids had done their sea training in *Berwick*, Cradock's flagship on the Mexican station in the autumn of 1913. He had always taken a great interest in junior officer training and made a habit of associating with the men on an informal basis. No doubt he now made his choices on the basis of considerable observation during that period.

The four appointments to *Good Hope* were dated August 17, 1914. The two ships met at sea, and the Admiral, his dog, his small staff, and the four midshipmen were transferred by boat. In the course of the evolution an irreplaceable Chinese vase that was the admiral's only valuable possession was accidentally broken. Captain Philip Francklin of *Suffolk* also exchanged places with the captain of *Good Hope*, so Admiral Cradock could continue to work with a flag captain he had come to know and trust.

The mids found themselves in their third ship in just two weeks: *Niobe, Suffolk,* and now *Good Hope.* Life on board was a far cry from the peacetime conditions to which they had been accustomed while under training. They had been warned not to bring any unnecessary items of clothing or personal effects. Like all ships on the outbreak of war, *Good Hope* had been stripped of her woodwork and furniture; nothing remained to soften the impact of the steel box in which they were enclosed.

In the days before radar and aerial or satellite surveillance the human eye was the only means of detecting an opponent. At night or in poor visibility the first warning might come with the enemy already at perilously close range. In peacetime, the ship's company was divided into three or even four watches for normal cruising; now they remained constantly at defence stations, with half the crew closed up at their guns during the hours of darkness. Those off watch slept in their clothes for quick response in the event of an alarm. There was no escaping the reality that they were at war and might at any moment be fighting for their lives.

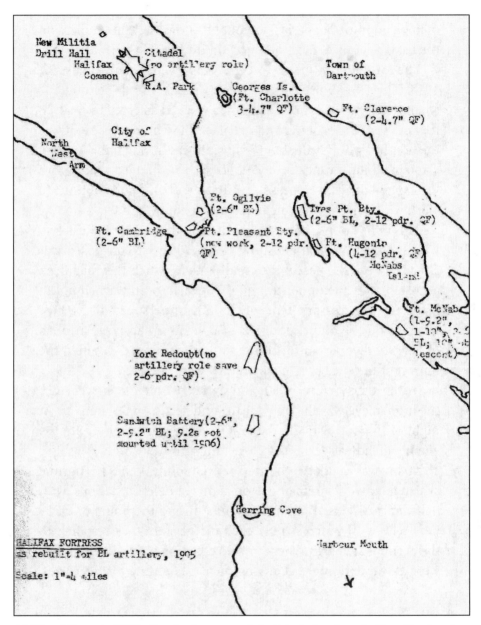

Halifax defences in 1905, after the departure of the British Garrison. In Canadian hands virtually no changes were made before August 1914 when war broke out. (Courtesy of Dr. Roger Sarty.)

NOTE
Halifax Coastal Defences

One counter-bombardment battery was at Fort McNab, mounting one 9.2- and one 10-inch breech loading gun. Fort McNab also covered the possible landing area at Lawrencetown. It mounted two concentrated-beam searchlights.

Its counterpart across the harbour was the Sandwich Battery, with two 9.2-inch and two 6-inch guns. A practice 12-pounder was also in the position, and just below the guns were two recently-installed concentrated-beam searchlights.

Fort Ives, located at the north end of McNabs Island, co-operated with Point Pleasant, Fort Charlotte, and Fort Clarence batteries in the close-in and inner roles. Equipped with two 6-inch and two 12-pounders, it also mounted five dispersed-beam searchlights to illuminate the inner channel narrows.

Fort Ogilvie was a close-in battery on the mainland opposite Ives Point, mounting two 6-inch guns.

Fort Clarence was an old position on the Dartmouth shore on what is now Imperial Oil property, an inner defence battery with two 4.7-inch guns.

Fort Charlotte on Georges Island was still equipped with long-outdated rifled muzzle-loaders and was not intended to be manned on mobilization. But on the insistence of the Royal Navy it was soon reactivated as an inner defence battery with three 4.7-inch guns.

Point Pleasant Battery at the southern end of the Halifax peninsula had once been abandoned, but was rebuilt and supple-mented the inner defences with two 12-pounder guns.

A few hundred yards south of Fort Ives was Fort Hugonin, armed with four 12-pounders. In co-operation with the Fort McNab 6-inch it covered the beaches below the batteries on the opposite shore of the harbour. It had a garrison of sixty officers and men, and was lit with kerosene, having no electricity supply.

CHAPTER SIX
Esquimalt Crisis,
August 1914

The Esquimalt Defence Scheme for the protection of the Victoria area had existed since 1902, its final version being approved in 1912–13. It was exercised every year.

As at Halifax, the navy's main commitment was the examination service. An area off Hatley Park was the designated examination anchorage; the supporting examination battery was sited at Black Rock. Examination officers and vessels were obtained from the merchant service.

The Canadian navy's west-coast intelligence centre was activated at the precautionary stage, as laid down in the War Book. By agreement it became the Royal Navy's only such station in the eastern Pacific, collecting information from an area stretching from the US–Mexican border to Honolulu, Midway Island, and north to the Bering Sea. All British consuls and agents on the American and Mexican west coasts passed reports to the centre.

As in the Atlantic, the navy's ability to carry out standard blue-water tasks was, of course, almost nonexistent. The obsolescent

From an unofficial start the Victoria company of the Royal Naval Canadian volunteer reserve evolved into the nationwide Royal Canadian Navy Volunteer Reserve.

Rainbow happened to be ready for sea in August 1914 only because she had been prepared to conduct the international Bering Strait seal protection patrol. Ready for sea she may have been, but she was far from ready for combat.

The Royal Navy still based two small ships at Esquimalt, the sloops *Shearwater* and *Algerine*, forty-nine and twenty-two years old, respectively. Armed with six 4-inch guns, they had the distinction of being propelled either by wind and sail or by steam, once the orders "up funnel, down screw, obey telegraphs" had been implemented. The sailing capability seems anachronistic, but it enabled them to remain at sea much longer, not being bound by the need to coal.

In the spring of 1914 both sloops were patrolling the west coast of Mexico, as part of the international monitoring of the Mexican Revolution.

The basic functions of the different types of coastal artillery were described in Chapter Four. The specific capabilities,

HMS Algerine, *Royal Navy sloop searched for by HMCS* Rainbow *in August 1914.*

location, and tactical features of the Esquimalt defences are outlined in the note on page 205.

As we know, at the outbreak of war the Esquimalt garrison consisted of units from both the permanent force and the active militia. The core was the 5th Company of Canadian regular garrison artillery with a strength of 112 officers and men. In peace it was supported by the specialized regular units outlined in Chapter Four. On mobilization, the fortress would be brought to wartime complement by the militia's 5th Regiment Canadian Garrison Artillery, with its strength of 390 officers and men. In addition, the newly created Duke of Connaught's Own Regiment of militia infantry was placed under the orders of the fortress commander. A Vancouver unit, at full establishment it would muster 306 all ranks.

For years British Columbia politicians had been complaining to Ottawa about the disgraceful inadequacy of military and naval defences on the west coast. Their pleas for help had gone largely unheard. In their vulnerable circumstances, and with a real threat on the horizon, it was natural that the political, military, and naval authorities overreacted as war became likely. Notwithstanding the well-practised Defence Scheme, mobilization was marked by political interference, hasty action, improvisation, and confusion.

As already noted, the official Warning Order had been issued on July 29. On August 1, using the lighthouse tender *Quadra*, the navy transferred a detachment of troops to Bamfield, on the west coast of Vancouver Island, where the vital trans-Pacific cable came ashore. They were followed by censors to monitor traffic on the ocean cable. On the same date the first detachment of fifty volunteers from the 5th Regiment were starting to reinforce the permanent garrison, and the navy stood up the examination service.

The declaration of war occurred at 3:00 p.m. local time August 4. By August 7 the militia artillerymen were fully mobilized. The unit's latest annual training camp had just ended with a firing competition against a towed target. The short-range Duntze Head battery scored 100 per cent hits with twenty rounds in thirty-five seconds; militia unit though it was, the 5th Regiment was far from amateurish when it counted.

Regimental mobilization orders directed every man "to provide himself with brushes, knife, fork spoon, and cup. These articles with a change of shirts, socks etc. will be carried in the valise canvas bags." Every shop window in Victoria displayed a printed mobilization card ordering members of the 5th to report at once to the Menzies Street Drill Hall. Handwritten underneath was the further instruction, "Bring a lunch."

Surprisingly, mobilization did not include the issue of uniforms; initially only a belt, a bayonet, and a haversack or valise were distributed. It was weeks before the men were fully kitted out, no doubt because volunteers proceeding overseas were given priority access to the limited stocks. Telephones were not in wide use at the time, and it was often days before the families of mobilized men knew where they were.

Numbers 1 and 2 companies of the 5th Regiment took over the Macaulay Point 6-inch battery (sixty-seven men), and manned the 12-pounder batteries at Duntze Head, Black Rock, and Belmont (ninety-five men in total). Number 3 Company of 120 men provided the mobile field force at Macaulay Point, armed with field guns and machine guns. The seventy-five-strong field force planned for Fort Rodd was to have come from the Duke of Connaught's Own, but only about forty men from this unit's authorized strength were actually available.

The 5th Regiment's headquarters staff and surplus men from Numbers 1 and 2 companies were concentrated at Work Point Barracks.

The regulars of the 5th Company were responsible for the two Rodd Hill batteries, requiring sixty-five officers and men. The unit also provided a few key personnel at each of the batteries assigned to the militia. Twenty-five men of the Royal Canadian Engineers were operating the searchlight systems at Fort Rodd and Black Rock. Garrison headquarters was on Signal Hill, along with eighteen specialists of the Canadian Ordnance Corps.

At mobilized strength the garrison should have mustered 57 officers and 815 men, totalling 872 all ranks. In the early days the actual number on the ground would have been about six hundred.

This information is compiled from a document in the 5th Regiment's archives, entitled "Distribution of Esquimalt Garrison and Active Militia." It makes no mention of the big-gun battery on Signal Hill, suggesting that it was not or could not be manned in the first days of mobilization. Possibly its designated gunners were still in Nanaimo, the last of the force to be stood down from riot duties. Apparently the counter-battery

HMCS Rainbow *ship's company in 1914. The crew was made up partly of regular seamen and partly of hastily enlisted volunteers. The latter group is probably in the dark uniforms, white uniforms not yet issued.*

capability of the Defence Scheme would not have been available had an attack occurred at the very outbreak of war. However, by August 12 the two Signal Hill 9.2-inch guns were operational and conducting firing practice.

Not only was the 5th Regiment mobilizing at Work Point Barracks but the newly raised British Columbia Horse and 88th regiments were recruiting, kitting out, and training at the same location. At times the situation must have bordered on the chaotic. The unit diary for the first days of the emergency is a curious document. Entries such as "Regiment manning Forts. Mobilized" receive no more emphasis than the faithful recording of daily band practice, or minutiae such as "No. 179 Gnr. Alexander took away Belt 189, Frog 189 and Pouch 189." A mere war was not going to disrupt the proper functioning of army life.

A curious unofficial unit made its appearance at this time. The Military District Commander received a letter from the Civil

Von Spee's East Asiatic Squadron contained two modern and powerful armoured cruisers, SMS Scharnhorst *(flagship) and* Gneisenau.

Service Drill and Rifle Association of Victoria, requesting that it be allowed to use the Menzies Street armoury for drill three nights a week. The request was quickly granted. The Association was still in existence and still training in 1915, and was listed as one of the Victoria volunteer units. The patriotic bureaucrats were never incorporated in the militia nor given a preassigned defence role, but would no doubt have given their best if called upon.

Such were the naval and military resources available at the outbreak of war. The threat they might have to face was a powerful German naval force in the Pacific.

As noted, Germany had been a latecomer to the nineteenth-century European scramble for colonies. Among the few she was able to acquire were some scattered islands in the Western Pacific, and the port of Tsingtao (now Qingdao) on the Shantung peninsula of China. With efficiency and hard work the place had been turned into an Asian version of a busy German town, and a first-class dockyard was constructed for the support of the East Asiatic Squadron, the only large force the German navy maintained outside home waters.

At its core were the two modern armoured cruisers *Scharnhorst* and *Gneisenau*. They were 11,600-ton sister ships, each mounting eight 8.2-inch and six 5.9-inch guns, with a top speed of 22.5 knots and a crew of 765. The squadron also consisted of the up-to-date light cruisers *Emden, Leipzig,* and *Nürnberg*, of the same class as *Dresden* and *Karlsruhe* in the Atlantic, plus some smaller coastal defence vessels. The men served two years on the station, half being rotated home each year in the commercial steamer that had carried their reliefs to Tsingtao. Most German sailors were conscripts doing their three years of compulsory service in the navy rather than in the army, but these crews were all long-service men. They were kept at a very high state of efficiency and training; the two big cruisers were the gunnery champions of the whole German navy.

A secondary task of the squadron was to look after German interests on the west coast of North America, and specifically to monitor the still-raging Mexican Revolution. In the spring of 1914 the ship on the Mexican station was *Leipzig*, destined to be the source of much concern and even panic in British Columbia.

The East Asiatic Squadron was commanded by the aggressive and intelligent Vice-Admiral Maximilian Graf (Count) von Spee, a gunnery expert who had entered the navy at the age of sixteen and risen rapidly through the officer ranks. His two sons were junior officers in the squadron. Churchill compared his isolated force to cut flowers in a vase: "beautiful to see, but doomed to die." Cut off from Germany though he was, von Spee could be depended upon to wreak maximum damage before the inevitable end.

On June 19, 1914, the East Asiatic Squadron had left Tsingtao for one of its routine tours of Germany's Far East possessions. The first port of call was Nagasaki, Japan. British naval weakness in the Far East had been more than offset by her 1902 alliance with Japan, which ensured that in any conflict the Japanese navy

CC-class submarine control room. Large handwheels control the angles of the forward and after planes.

would be brought into the scales against von Spee. It must have been with sober thoughts that the visiting Germans measured the power of the Japanese battleships that were their Nagasaki hosts.

On June 22 von Spee's ships anchored at the island of Saipan, purchased from Spain in 1899. As usual the squadron coaled from the accompanying commercial colliers, a brutal task especially in the tropics. A few days later von Spee received startling news from Europe: the Archduke Franz Ferdinand had been assassinated. The routine cruise began to assume a new complexion.

For the next month the East Asiatic Squadron moved among the German island colonies, coaling as often as possible. On July 9 von Spee received a German Admiralty appreciation predicting that the Triple Alliance would indeed become involved in the escalating crisis, and two days later he was warned that British neutrality had become problematic. The Alert Message, "Threatened State of War," was issued July 30, one day later than the Warning Telegram, its British equivalent. The alert was the signal for the German ships to prepare for action by landing all personal effects, including the many souvenirs the men had acquired. Wooden articles and woodwork stripped from cabins and messes were thrown overboard. Von Spee visited each ship in turn. Standing in front of a gun turret, he exhorted his men to make good their oaths to the fatherland. News of the British declaration of war reached him on August 6.

The question was how to employ his very powerful force. The German naval staff left the decision to the man on the spot. Von Spee conceived that his mission was to inflict economic injury consistent with international law, and prevent or delay the transport of enemy troops and supplies, while forcing the allies to divert resources to search for his squadron. He would fight only if enemy forces tried to interfere with that mission.

None of von Spee's strategic alternatives were attractive. Japanese and British forces in Far East waters would overwhelm him if he attempted to defend Tsingtao and the other German possessions. Troop convoys from India, Australia, and New Zealand to France were high-value targets, but well-escorted by forces superior to his own. In the end, the least bad option seemed to be to operate against the undefended allied trade on the west coast of America, especially South America, where no British ships were stationed. In Chile especially he had numerous sources of intelligence and opportunities to charter colliers to replenish his vital coal supplies; with its large German immigrant population he could count on a good reception at the port of Valparaiso. As he expressed it;

> *If we were to proceed toward the coast of*
> [South] *America we should have both coaling*
> *ports and agents at our disposal, and the Japanese*
> *fleet could not follow us thither without causing*
> *great concern in the United States and so*
> *influencing that country in our favour.*

Before the war the light cruiser *Leipzig* had been detached to the Mexican patrol. In mid-July von Spee sent *Nürnberg* to Honolulu, to deliver and collect mail before rejoining. As it happened, *Nürnberg* had previously been stationed in Mexican waters. After departing Honolulu on the twenty-ninth she vanished from British intelligence; the possibility that she was on her way to join *Leipzig* could not be ruled out.

The threat triggered widespread alarm on the west coast. The war brought out a wave of patriotic enthusiasm and men enlisted by the hundreds, but some inhabitants prepared to flee inland. The Victoria *Daily Colonist* helpfully published an article on the international law of bombardment, triggering a rush to purchase bombardment insurance policies. Concerned about the possibility of a ransom demand, many banks shipped their gold to Winnipeg or Seattle, and arranged to burn their paper currency. Women and children were ordered to leave their married quarters in the Esquimalt yard, and work began on converting the liner *Prince George* to a hospital ship.

Rainbow's part in the *Komagata Maru* affair was described in Chapter Four. Returning to Esquimalt on July 25, she docked to have her copper sheathing cleaned. On August 2 the Royal Canadian Navy and the Naval Volunteer Force were placed on active service, and she embarked a total of seventy-six men from the Vancouver and Victoria companies of volunteers.

War not having been declared, *Rainbow* was not yet under the operational control of the Admiralty. However, at its request, on August 1 Naval Service Headquarters addressed a secret message to Commander Hose:

> *Prepare for active service trade protection*
> *grain ships going south. German cruiser* Nürnberg
> *or* Leipzig *is on west coast America. Obtain all*
> *information available as to merchant ships sailing*

*from Canadian or U.S. ports. Telegraph demands
for ordnance stores required to complete to fullest
capacity. Urgent.*

He was also ordered to meet the special ammunition train
expected to arrive from Halifax by August 6 carrying high-
explosive rounds. In the meantime *Rainbow* carried only solid
practice shot and a very few rounds of outdated common shell
filled with gunpowder rather than high explosives. Her radio
had a range of only two hundred miles, although this was later
much improved through the ingenuity of her wireless operators. She was fully coaled, but no accompanying collier would
be available, and no guaranteed coaling source existed south of
Esquimalt. The attitude of the neutral United States was yet to
be determined.

At 1 a.m. on August 3 the sole west coast unit of the RCN
sailed to the south, maintaining wireless contact with the station at Patchena on the southwest point of Vancouver Island.
The superintendent of the dockyard wrote, ". . . but few of those
who saw her depart on that eventful occasion expected to see her
return." At 8:07 the following morning the commanding officer
received a message informing him that war had been declared.
Rainbow thus became the first ship of the Royal Canadian Navy
ever to be at sea as a belligerent. Now under the operational control of the British Admiralty, Commander Hose was instructed
to proceed to Vancouver to meet the special ammunition train.
En route the ship carried out firing exercises with both 6- and
4.7-inch guns, using the solid-shot practice rounds.

Two days later he had reached the Race Rock light near
Esquimalt when his orders were changed. Hose was directed
to once again steer south to meet and escort to safety the Royal
Navy sloops *Algerine* and *Shearwater*, returning from their
Mexican mission. Either or both together would have been

Rainbow *sailing from Esquimalt. Early in the war she was dispatched to counter German raiders, which would probably have sunk her if contact had ever been made.*

easy prey for one of the German cruisers. Organizing a rendezvous would be difficult since neither was fitted with wireless. *Rainbow*'s captain was speeded on his way by a Naval Service Headquarters' message:

> Nürnberg *and* Leipzig *reported August 4th off Magdalena Bay steering north. Do your utmost to protect* Algerine *and* Shearwater, *steering north from San Diego. Remember Nelson and the British Navy. All Canada is watching.*

By design or not, the wording managed to capture both the imperialist and the nationalist conceptions of Canada's place in the world.

At the outbreak of war *Shearwater* was off Ensenada, Mexico, not far south of San Diego. *Algerine* was further south at Mazatlan with an international observation force. In addition to *Leipzig* the force also consisted of the Japanese heavy cruiser *Idzumo*, as well as American vessels. At the end of July the group had collaborated in the evacuation of their nationals as the rebels prepared to storm the town. As was common before the war, friendly relations were established between the German and British ships; at a personal level the officers of the two navies always got on very well with each other.

The Germans had chartered the Vancouver-registered collier *Cetriana*. Her master was an officer of the Royal Naval Reserve. On July 31 she arrived at Mazatlan to transfer coal and other supplies to *Leipzig*. On arrival, her crew was replaced by new seamen, mostly Germans and Mexicans.

On August 5 *Leipzig*'s Captain Johannes Hahn learned of the declaration of war. In order of priority, his tasks were to rejoin von Spee's squadron, to disrupt commercial trade, and to engage enemy warships. Before rejoining he wished to safeguard his fuel supplies by coaling and, if possible, chartering a collier to accompany him on his subsequent movements. He decided to make for San Francisco. At this time both British sloops and the Japanese cruiser were also moving north by different routes. Although *Algerine* must have been in Hahn's near vicinity at some point it does not appear that he tried very hard to find her. On August 6 he learned from the San Diego marine radio that *Rainbow* and two submarines were at Esquimalt; of course, he had no way of assessing their combat readiness.

***

At dawn on August 5, with *Rainbow* newly embarked on her first wartime mission, an unlikely pair of men peered from the entrance to Esquimalt harbour into the morning mists of the Strait of Juan de Fuca. One was Sir Richard McBride, premier of British Columbia, the other Lieutenant H.B. Pilcher, Royal Navy, of Her Majesty's Canadian Ship *Rainbow*, left ashore as Senior Naval Officer in the absence of Commander Hose. This young man had been managing the confusion of mobilization when he found himself the Senior Naval Officer, immersed in a tangled intrigue involving politics, international relations, commercial business, and high finance, dealing as an equal with important men whom he would probably never have met under normal circumstances. He was worn out both physically and mentally.

The two were awaiting the outcome of an astonishingly daring plan, already unfolding, and shrouded in secrecy. Success would for a short time make British Columbia the only Canadian province with a navy, while tripling the number of Canadian warships on the west coast. Failure would mean personal disgrace and would trigger a dispute with the United States, with consequences that could not be foreseen. As they waited both men must have mentally retraced the trail of events that had brought them to this place and time.

In 1911 the Chilean Navy had commissioned the Seattle Construction and Drydock Company to construct two C-class submarines, using plans provided by the Electric Boat Company of Connecticut, a builder of similar craft for the USN. They were to be named *Iquique* and *Antofagasta*. Having been launched in 1913, by the spring of 1914 they were virtually completed, but after sea trials the Chileans were complaining that the boats had insufficient range and were too heavy. Crews were in Seattle ready to take them over, but the Chilean government had stopped making progress payments to the Electric Boat Company, which in turn had stopped payments to its Seattle subcontractor. The Chileans therefore had no legal claim to ownership, although they subsequently argued unsuccessfully to the contrary.

On July 27 James V. Paterson, President of Seattle Construction and Drydock, visited Victoria and later Vancouver. With war clearly on the horizon he saw a business opportunity to sell the two submarines to Canada from under the noses of the troublesome Chileans. He was soon in contact with Captain W.H. Logan of

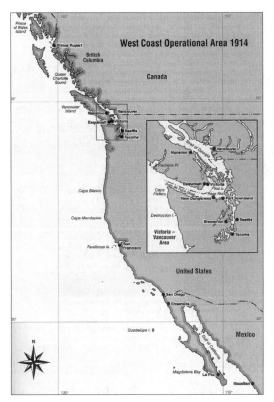

West Coast Operational Area 1914

HMCS Rainbow *operating area. In the first month of the war the ship steamed 4,500 nautical miles, responding to alerts.*

Victoria, a marine surveyor for the London Salvage Association. Logan was well aware of the Chilean situation, and quickly recognized the potential benefits to Canada.

On July 29, a group of prominent citizens lunched in Victoria's Union Club, among them Logan and Paterson, on a second visit. The latter let it be known that the submarines were for sale, and then he returned to Seattle. Logan brought the matter to the attention of Premier McBride. As we saw in Chapter Three, Sir Richard was extremely concerned about the safety of his defenceless province, and was also well aware of the deterrent value of submarines. He contacted Admiral Kingsmill, and by the next day the latter was attempting to identify qualified submariners, although the purchase was still no more than an idea.

It happened that the Federal Minister of Agriculture Martin Burrell was staying with the Member of Parliament for Victoria, G.H. Barnard. At the request of the premier the two parliamentarians met with Captain Logan on Saturday, August 1, soon adjourning to the dockyard to seek naval advice on the acquisition.

Sir Richard McBride, activist premier of British Columbia in WWI. He was instrumental in the acquisition of Canada's first submarines, and constantly intervened in defence issues affecting British Columbia.

Captain Hose was about to sail and very busy, so Lieutenant Pilcher was interviewed. The young lieutenant advised the group that the submarines would indeed be of great benefit to the defences. Armed with this professional opinion, albeit from a very junior officer, the group reported to the premier and further discussions went on over the weekend.

With war imminent action became urgent. At 3 p.m. Monday, August 3, a meeting was held in the dockyard, interrupted at times while Logan and Paterson conferred on the telephone. The latter agreed to sell the boats for a price of $575,000 each, the equivalent of approximately twenty-five times as much today. Shocked, Logan attempted to bargain, but Paterson answered brusquely, "This is no time to indulge in talk of that kind, and I will not listen to it, if you do not care to take the boats you do not need to take them." The price to have been paid by Chile was $818,000 for both boats, but in the circumstances Paterson's outrageous offer could not be refused. Paterson did agree to move the boats to the international boundary in Juan de Fuca Strait, to be handed over to the Canadians on presentation of a government cheque for $1,150,000. Lieutenant Pilcher then signed off on the following naval message, which was encoded and dispatched:

> *Naval, Ottawa, Ont. — Esquimalt B.C., Aug. 3, 1914*
>
> *Two submarines actually completed for Chilean government Seattle, estimated cost $1,150,000 could probably purchase; ready for action, torpedoes on board. Chilean government cannot take possession. Provincial government will advance money pending remittance.*

Then the waiting began. In Seattle Paterson made preparations for sailing, hiring nine of the earlier Chilean trials team for each boat, under Lieutenant-Commander S.B. Smith, a retired United States Navy officer. The men were not told of their destination. Meanwhile, shipyard workers made minor adjustments to the equipment. They were not informed of the reasons, but the nature of the last-minute activities must have made some suspect that the boats were being prepared for sea. Although many Chileans were also working onboard their suspicions were not aroused.

Paterson strongly desired to carry out the operation on the night of August 3, and was ready to do so. That afternoon he sent a telegram to Logan, again advising that he needed to be paid by government cheque, and urging immediate action. To this Logan could only reply:

> *Awaiting Federal decision. Don't move until you hear further from me tonight. Apparently everything alright.*

Thus made aware that an August 3 departure was out of the question, Paterson was faced with the problem of maintaining secrecy for at least another day. Miraculously, although the passage crews were partially in on the secret there was no leakage of information; the Chileans remained in the dark.

The Admiralty had been asked for an assessment of the capabilities of the Chilean boats. Until this was received, there would be no Federal decision, although behind the scenes at Naval Service Headquarters contingency plans were being made in the hope of a positive reply.

To save time, at some point on August 3 Premier McBride decided to make all preparations for the acquisition should it be approved. He signed a Province of British Columbia cheque for the purchase amount, carried by hand of trusted government messenger, a Mr. Ryan, to Lieutenant Pilcher at the dockyard. The harried Pilcher had identified two key personnel to actually conduct the transfer. One was Lieutenant Bertram Jones, who less than two years before had commanded a British C-Class boat, before retiring and immigrating to British Columbia. Being on the Royal Navy's Emergency List he volunteered for service as the crisis worsened, and was immediately enrolled in the Royal Canadian Navy.

As Acting Senior Naval Officer, Lieutenant Pilcher gave him written orders to proceed in the civilian tug *Salvor* to a position five miles south of Trial Island, where two submarines would be met. He was to inspect them, and if he considered them worth the agreed price he was to hand the cheque over to Paterson and bring the boats to Esquimalt. Jones would carry the cheque. He was joined by Chief Engineering Artificer R.H. Wood, the Chief Engineer of the Dockyard. These two, along with Ryan, were to sail on the evening of the fourth to meet the submarines at the international boundary. One source states that several naval artificers and sailors also accompanied the inspection party.

The premier now formally advised Naval Service Headquarters that the operation was proceeding.

> *After consultation with Burrell and naval*
> *officers have advanced tonight one million one*
> *hundred and fifty thousand dollars to Lieut. Pilcher,*
> *senior naval officer in command, for purchase*
> *two modern submarines lying Seattle harbour*
> *and built for Chile. All arrangements complete for*
> *their arrival Esquimalt tomorrow morning unless*
> *untoward incident occurs. Congratulate Canada*
> *if this operation successful on acquisition of such*
> *useful adjunct defence of country.*

The statement "All arrangements complete for their arrival Esquimalt" would turn out to be extremely inaccurate, with near-disastrous consequences.

In the absence of formal approval the premier had overstepped his jurisdiction and assumed an awesome responsibility that could be justified only by success.

***

Logan travelled to Seattle on the morning of August 4, the transfer being scheduled for that night. He did not travel alone. At a parade of the Naval Volunteer Force a certain Able-Seaman Brown was called from the ranks and summoned to an interview with the premier. Other than being a keen weekend sailor his qualifications are unknown. At the time Seattle was supposed to be alive with German spies, and Brown may have been charged with evaluating the dependability of the passage crews and identifying any who might be prepared to serve with the Canadian navy after the transfer. In neutral America he travelled in civilian clothes, and according to Logan "looked like a hobo"; another source says he was dressed as a chef.

At 2 p.m. Logan and Brown disembarked from the ferry at Seattle and were met by Paterson. By this time it was known that the British government had issued an ultimatum requiring the Germans to withdraw its troops from Belgium. War would be declared if a satisfactory reply was not received by 12:00 p.m. Berlin time, 3:00 p.m. Pacific time. In that event, it was believed that President Wilson would sign the American *Neutrality Act* the following day, and the submarine transfer would become an offence under that statute. Thus, the boats had to make their clandestine departure on the night of the fourth. Although there was still no reply from the Admiralty and hence no federal decision, Premier McBride had taken responsibility for going ahead, and Logan acted accordingly. He spent the afternoon trying unsuccessfully to recruit ex-United States Navy submariners, while Brown mingled with the passage crews.

As night descended the crews boarded the submarines. Logan, Paterson, and Smith were in the *Antofagasta,* and Brown in the *Iquique.* Port clearance had not been requested or obtained. Whether they knew it or not, by this time Canada was officially at war. About 10 p.m. lines were let go. In a light fog and without showing navigation lights the boats steered for the harbour entrance on the surface, using battery power rather than their noisy diesel engines. The American coastal artillery emplacements were passed without incident. Diesels were started and course was set for the rendezvous with Canadian authorities, still on the surface. Later the cruiser USS *Milwaukee* was sent in pursuit, but never sighted the fugitives.

***

The rendezvous was a position five miles south of Trial Island. This was on the American side of the international boundary bisecting the Strait of Juan de Fuca, but two miles outside that country's three-mile limit. At dawn the submarines were in position, but there was no sign of the tug bringing the Canadian party. At this point a Seattle-bound liner passed nearby. To avoid suspicion the boats set a course parallel to the boundary until the liner was out of sight.

About 5 a.m. the *Salvor* was sighted and the three vessels were soon alongside each other. Paterson was anxious to complete the transaction expeditiously, but Jones insisted on carrying out an inspection of both boats. He and Wood were meticulous in visiting every corner of the vessels, even having the battery covers lifted for examination. After two hours Jones was satisfied, and indeed impressed. He passed the cheque to Paterson but insisted on a receipt that had to be scribbled on an envelope he happened to have in his pocket. At that point small white ensigns were hoisted on the conning towers, all present gave three cheers for the King, and the tug and submarines got under way for Esquimalt.

On Duntze Head McBride and Pilcher continued to wait, their anxiety at fever pitch. Visibility was limited by heat haze. Without warning the silence was broken by the shrieking whistle of the unarmed vessel *Malaspina*, then on duty at the examination anchorage. She had sighted two unidentified submarines, and now raced for the harbour with her siren lanyard lashed to the rail, signalling frantically in almost unreadable semaphore. At this point the two watchers must have come to the shocking realization that secrecy had been carried too far, and that they were the only people in Esquimalt who were aware of British Columbia's new navy. Disaster loomed.

The *Malaspina* did not matter, but the examination battery at Black Rock did. The battery's militia gunners were extremely proficient, regularly scoring 100 per cent hits in target practice. Now the 12-pounder crews were looking at two specks on the horizon that were apparently intent on penetrating the harbour, and began tracking the targets while awaiting the order to open fire. The battery signal sergeant interpreted the *Malaspina*'s signalling to mean "two German cruisers coming." On this the battery commander, Captain A.E. Craddock, alerted all manned batteries. Three 6-inch and six 12-pounder guns were ready to engage on the first shot from Black Rock. The fire command post alerted the dockyard, to receive the reply, "My God, what do we do now?"

Meanwhile, using semaphore, the battery commander had ordered the signal sergeant to request the boats to identify themselves, only to be informed that "They are waving their hands, Sir."

The cool-headed Craddock continued to observe and at length was able to make out the white ensigns on the conning towers as well as the people waving from the decks. There was a chance that the submarines were reinforcements falsely rumoured to be coming from Hong Kong. He withheld fire, leaving the Duntze Head gunners at the narrowest point of the channel to make the final decision, as the intruders passed them at point-blank range. At that time all doubts were removed, the boats were accepted as friendly, and the batteries stood down after a very realistic test of their readiness — and a close call with a political and military disaster.

By 8 a.m. the submarines were secured in the dockyard and the premier was being briefed by Jones and Logan. The near-disastrous arrival and accumulated stress triggered Lieutenant Pilcher's complete breakdown. He signalled Naval Service Headquarters recommending that the two submarines be christened *Paterson* and *McBride*, and promoted Brown to Sub-Lieutenant, all the while issuing a stream of orders to which no one paid any attention. He was examined the next day by the senior medical officer, who pronounced him unfit for duty. He was later recalled to Britain. He does not seem to have received any official recognition for his efforts under unprecedented circumstances.

On returning to his office Premier McBride read a Naval Service Headquarters telegram dispatched at 8:20 a.m. Pacific time. It read, "Prepare to purchase submarines, telegraph price." With the boats already alongside, the exasperated premier replied, "Have prepared, purchased submarines." Prime Minister Borden later sent a more positive message, saying, ". . . we appreciate most warmly your action, which will tend to increase security on the Pacific coast, and send hearty thanks."

At some point on this busy day a hasty inquiry into the surprise call to action was conducted by Major Ogilvie of the Military District staff. The premier and Lieutenant Pilcher were on the metaphorical hot seat. They were of course unable to justify their failure to notify the artillery commanders of their plans, but it was judged that further proceedings would serve no purpose.

On August 7 the Dominion reimbursed British Columbia for the purchase price, and incorporated the boats into the Royal Canadian Navy. At the same time they were transferred to the operational control of the Admiralty. Pilcher's suggested names were rejected in favour of the Royal Navy's two-character system for submarines, a letter indicating the class — in this case "C" — followed by a sequence number within the class. To indicate Canadian ownership, the usual two characters were preceded by another "C"; the boats were thus named His Majesty's Canadian Submarines *CC1* and *CC2*.

The shrewd businessman Paterson hastened to deposit his payment. He had accurately gauged the desperation of his Canadian customers and had exacted a price well in excess of the Chilean contract. The Electric Boat and Seattle Drydock companies were entirely satisfied, and hidden in the total amount was a $40,000 commission to Paterson for his efforts.

Submarine CC2 at sea.

In *Canada's Submariners, 1914–1923,* Dave Perkins recounts the tale of a planned second clandestine operation even more daring than the one just completed. Premier McBride's triumph was marred by the news that, contrary to previous information, the boat's torpedoes were not on board, but held in Seattle. *Rainbow* carried torpedoes, but they were 14-inch and not 18-inch as in the two submarines.

The invaluable Captain Logan volunteered or was persuaded to undertake a second raid to obtain the weapons, well aware that the American authorities would now be on full alert. He learned that the Chileans had custody of two torpedoes, fitted with practice warheads only but capable of being upgraded to warshots. Travelling to Seattle, he determined that they were well guarded, but persuaded the senior Chilean officer to relax his precautions.

To quote Dave Perkins:

> *He also made arrangements to acquire the*
> *gyroscopes, primers and detonators (the latter two*
> *were needed for converting the practice heads into*
> *warheads), which were held in Paterson's office.*

*Returning to the shed where they were kept Logan
prepared the weapons for transport, hired a fast
power launch, and engaged a pilot to spirit him
and his charges back to Canadian waters.*

McBride had probably neglected to advise Ottawa of his new initiative. On the brink of implementation, Logan's plan was inadvertently jeopardized by the intervention of Naval Service Headquarters. The Deputy Minister of Naval Affairs sent an open telegram to Paterson's firm offering to purchase torpedoes. His message was intercepted by the United States Navy, which placed the shipyard under guard. Incredibly, Logan still stood ready to break in and steal the warhead fittings. But by this time it was known that *Niobe*'s torpedoes were the same size as the those of the submarines, and could be shipped from Halifax immediately. The risks now far outweighed the potential rewards, and Premier McBride wisely called the operation off.

Everyone involved at the Seattle end was assuming a heavy risk. Logan's daring plan must have been lubricated with significant sums of money. The Canadian navy was almost certainly not the source, as shown by the deputy minister's apparent ignorance of what was going on. Whether or not provincial finances were secretly tapped again will probably never be known.

The submarines were in Esquimalt, but they were a long way from being operationally ready. Nothing could be accomplished without crews. Having supervised the transfer, Lieutenant Jones would have been an ideal choice to take command and attract recruits by any means short of the press gang. But Lieutenant Pilcher's breakdown meant that a replacement temporary Senior Naval Officer was needed, and the choice fell on Jones.

By great good fortune, a well-qualified substitute was available. Adrian Keyes had commanded two Royal Navy submarines before retiring. At this time his later very famous brother Roger

Keyes was head of the British submarine service. Adrian immigrated to Canada, and was living in Toronto when war became probable. Being on the Emergency List he reported for duty, and on July 30 was unexpectedly interviewed by Rear-Admiral Kingsmill himself, who was already aware of the still-secret submarine acquisition project. Accompanied by another former Royal Navy officer, also recruited by Kingsmill, Keyes was soon on a westbound train, arriving in Esquimalt on the morning of August 5, where he became "Officer in Command of Submarines" as well as commanding officer of *CC1*. When *Shearwater* returned to Esquimalt her crew was sent to Halifax to help man *Niobe*. Her captain became Senior Naval Officer, and Jones took command of *CC2*.

*****

Each submarine required a crew of nineteen, including three officers: captain, first lieutenant and third hand. Keyes chose the thirty-two other ranks at a parade, concentrating on a few submarine-related trades or qualifications. The selectees included nine British and Canadian regulars, including two with submarine experience, and twenty-three almost entirely untrained Canadian Volunteer Reservists. Their escape training consisted of donning a self-contained breathing apparatus and walking from the shallow to the deep end of a Victoria swimming pool before rising to the surface. Training began with an all-out effort by each individual to become familiar with the location and purpose of the numerous unfamiliar systems and equipment.

Midshipman William Maitland-Dougall was a member of the first class to graduate from the Royal Naval College of Canada. He was on leave at his parent's home in Duncan, B.C., when he and his classmates were ordered to report to the nearest naval unit; Esquimalt dockyard, in his case. Here he would have encountered

C-class submarine's torpedo compartment, or fore ends. Note inner ends of tubes near deck level.

the overworked Lieutenant Pilcher, who would have had no idea what to do with him. Thus, he was on the dock when the submarines arrived, and soon found himself the third hand of *CC1*. His first task was to trace all the boat's systems and arrange for the numerous Spanish labels to be replaced by English equivalents.

The boats began by diving alongside in slow time, gradually progressing to standard dives in deep water, coached initially by a retired American officer provided by the Electric Boat Company. It soon appeared that Chilean complaints about the boats might indeed have some validity, as they showed a tendency to unexpectedly assume acute bow-down or stern-down angles. On one occasion *CC1* was dived with a good trim off Hatley Park when she suddenly took on a steep bow-down angle and headed for the bottom. The American officer ordered "Full ahead both and blow bow main ballast!" Keyes immediately over-ruled him by ordering, "Full astern both and blow all main ballast!" His order was obeyed and the boat was brought under control.

The crews were soon practising dummy torpedo launches from the surface, aiming at Dallas Road on the Victoria waterfront, to the delight of the crowds that gathered to watch. At midnight August 9 a special train had left Halifax with nine 18-inch war torpedoes configured for surface discharge. On arrival they needed minor modifications to fit the submarines' tubes. One was damaged in the process, but *CC1* received five and *CC2* three of those that remained; for unexplained reasons the Chileans had designed the two boats to have a different number of tubes. Defects caused by shoddy construction would continue to require rectification, but the newly armed boats could now be considered combat-ready, capable of playing a part in defence of the fortress and the Strait of Juan de Fuca.

The following incident illustrates the rather unorthodox approach already becoming a characteristic of the submarine service. Keyes had driven the inexperienced crews very hard to produce efficient fighting units as quickly as possible. Until this was achieved he refused to grant leave. In response the sailors made plans for a false wedding, a petty officer putting himself forward as the supposed groom. They surmised that on such an occasion their commander could hardly refuse to grant leave for the afternoon and evening, and indeed he did not. As a participant wrote, "The next problem was to procure a bride and bridesmaids. Not a difficult matter in Victoria, and a most glorious party ensued." The wedding dinner was held in the popular Westholm Grill. Several submarine officers dining there separately noted the festivities, including the suitably costumed bride and bridesmaids. Leave expired at 1:00 a.m.

Keyes himself was not amused. Just three hours later, at 4 a.m., he took both boats to sea in very heavy weather. As Keyes expressed it, "They have had their wedding dinner; now I will give the beggars their wedding breakfast."

***

The deterrent value of the submarines was enhanced when the United States Navy warned all American shipping that Canadian submarines were operating in coastal waters. According to the German official history *Leipzig* did steam as far north as Cape Flattery but did not enter Juan de Fuca Strait. The decision not to proceed may well have been influenced by the unseen menace of the submarines. In a few short months *Leipzig* and her log and other records would be at the bottom of the sea, and her captain dead. The truth will probably never be known.

CC1 and *CC2* were extremely cramped, and constantly permeated by fumes. Sanitary arrangements were rudimentary, and most men slept on the battery tops due to a lack of bunks. Cooking facilities consisted of an electric stovetop on which meals were sometimes cooked by an untrained sailor and usually served cold. Constant alertness was required. Even a few days on patrol under these harsh conditions placed severe stress on the ship's companies, stress that had to be relieved in harbour. The former Royal Navy sloop *Shearwater* was therefore recommissioned into the Canadian navy and became the submarine depot ship, providing food, accommodation and ablution facilities between patrols. Her amenities were limited, but like day and night compared to conditions in the boats. In addition she had workshop facilities and acted as the target when the boats practiced submerged attacks and dummy torpedo firings. She also accompanied the boats on their occasional visits to Vancouver in support of civilian morale.

***

We left *Rainbow* on August 6, bent on her mission to escort *Algerine* and *Shearwater* to safety under threat of the German cruiser *Leipzig*. Had the two met the outcome would scarcely have been in doubt. The range of the Canadian ship's 6-inch guns was

Personnel of His Majesty's Canadian Submarine CC1. Shown are Lt.-Cmdr. Adrian Keyes, RN, centre, and Midshipman William Maitland-Dougall, RCN, lower right. Before the war's end Maitland-Dougall was killed while in command of a British submarine.

less than half that of the *Leipzig*'s modern 4.1-inch weapons, and the rate of fire much slower. Moreover, she had still not picked up her high-explosive ammunition. The German ship's speed advantage (25 as compared with 17 knots) would have allowed her to remain out of range while systematically destroying her opponent. Her crack crew were experienced and extremely well trained, while *Rainbow* was well under complement, even including the large number of volunteers with little or no training.

But the situation was not as grim as many observers believed. *Rainbow*'s mission did not necessarily involve seeking battle with a stronger opponent; it was simply to rescue the sloops. To avoid detection the commanding officer intended to take advantage of the fog so prevalent off San Francisco. In low visibility there was a chance that she could damage *Leipzig* by an early shot at close range if they did meet, which would have been a disaster for *Leipzig* because there was no possibility of repair short of Germany. Captain Hahn had no way of knowing the parlous state of *Rainbow*'s armament and crew. The aim of the German captain was not to seek battle, but to disrupt the north–south trade. He might even capture or sink one of the famous Canadian Pacific liners that maintained service between Vancouver and Australia.

On August 7 it was definitely reported that *Nürnberg* had joined *Leipzig*; only much later was it realized that the report was wrong. *Rainbow* arrived at San Francisco on the same day. The Americans were extremely protective of their neutral status, and it was only with considerable difficulty that the British Consul General persuaded them to allow the cruiser to embark fifty tons of coal. Late in the evening the Consul General informed Commander Hose that one or both German ships were off the harbour entrance. *Rainbow* sailed at midnight. Although it was not part of his mission Hose believed that, being aware of their presence, it was now his duty to make contact.

At 2 a.m. on the eighth a lifesaving station reported that *Rainbow* was laid-to just outside the three-mile limit. The ship was rather belatedly jettisoning unneeded furniture and flammable material. The debris drifted in to the Golden Gate, triggering a report that *Rainbow* had been destroyed, temporarily causing much gloom in Victoria. *Rainbow* continued for some days to lurk in the vicinity of the Farallon Islands, about eighty miles off San Francisco; throughout the period the Island wireless station continued to report her position. On August 10 shortage of coal forced her to turn north for Esquimalt. The next day the Canadian Press confirmed from San Francisco that on the tenth the ship had been off Cape Mendocino, 195 miles north of San Francisco.

The next day *Leipzig* reached the Farallones, where the German Consul arrived by boat and informed Captain Hahn that he had not yet been able to obtain permission for the ship to coal. Hahn decided to return on the seventeenth and enter the port unless otherwise instructed. In the meantime he would interdict trade off the Golden Gate before steaming north to engage *Rainbow*.

Submarines CC1 *and* CC2 *alongside in Esquimalt under repair, or possibly during construction in Seattle.*

***

Leipzig ranged as far north as Cape Mendocino. Between August 11 and 13, *Rainbow* was in the same waters, probably always north of the enemy. On the twelfth she spotted a suspected warship to the south, assumed to be *Leipzig*. Well aware of his ship's inferiority, Captain Hose altered course away to bring the after 6-inch gun to bear on her presumed pursuer. The stranger turned out to be the hastily converted hospital ship *Prince George*, which had been sent after *Rainbow* in anticipation of the cruiser's defeat. She conveyed a message ordering Hose to return to base to embark his ammunition, the delayed special train having arrived.

En route *Rainbow* met *Shearwater* at the entrance to the Strait of Juan de Fuca. Her captain was greatly concerned for the safety of *Algerine*, but had no information as to her position. However, *Prince George* soon reported sighting the sloop off the northern California coast. Having coaled and embarked the replacement ammunition, *Rainbow* once again sailed to find her. Morale was high, but plunged when it was discovered that the new shells lacked fuses, rendering them useless. After this blow it was a relief when *Algerine* was at length discovered, lying stopped and using one of her boats to transfer coal from a commandeered collier. Her captain messaged, "I am damn glad to see you," as well he might be, and the two ships set off for home, arriving in Esquimalt on August 15, where *Rainbow* finally received the essential fuses.

On the seventeenth *Leipzig* entered San Francisco and began to coal, but had to stop because proper permission had not yet been granted. Under international rules she could embark only sufficient fuel to reach the nearest German port. This was deemed to be Apia, Samoa, the American authorities seemingly unaware that the place had been captured by the New Zealanders on the outbreak of war. In any case, the quantity allowed was ample for Captain Hahn's purposes, which were to interdict trade while gradually moving southward.

He had already been heading south when, with her unfused Lyddite shells, *Rainbow* set off to locate *Algerine*; there was no chance of an encounter on this occasion. After August 18 there was no news of *Leipzig*'s whereabouts for more than a month.

On August 19 an unidentified three-funnel cruiser was reported to be near the totally undefended port of Prince Rupert. Setting out at once, *Rainbow* reached Prince Rupert on the twenty-first. Inquiries tended to substantiate the rumour, Hose signalling on the twenty-third, "Strong suspicions *Nürnberg* or *Leipzig* has coaled from U.S. Steamship *Delhi* in vicinity of Prince of Wales Island on Aug. 19th or Aug. 20th." The suspicions were never confirmed, and the strange ship was certainly not a German cruiser. Rumours such as this one were rife on both coasts, and repeatedly induced great confusion in the operational picture. By the time *Rainbow* returned to Esquimalt on September 2 she had

German light cruiser Leipzig *coaling in San Francisco, August 1914. HMCS* Rainbow *searched for her but never made contact.*

steamed more than 4,300 nautical miles in a month.

As we have seen, the multinational collection of ships monitoring developments off Mexico also included the Japanese armoured cruiser *Idzumo*. On the outbreak of war *Leipzig* had begun moving north. With Japan still neutral, *Idzumo* proceeded in the same direction, not in contact with the German ship, but generally following her movements. On August 23 Japan at last fulfilled her alliance obligations by declaring war on Germany, and two days later *Idzumo* entered Esquimalt dockyard, thereby doubling the number of surface ships in the local naval force. The *Vancouver Sun* saw fit to note that *Idzumo*'s assistance was welcome, but that it would not influence British Columbia's long-standing opposition to Asian immigration. The naval force received further reinforcement on August 30, when His Majesty's Ship *Newcastle* arrived from Hong Kong.

Rainbow was inferior to *Leipzig*, but the new arrivals reversed the situation. *Idzumo* was a powerful vessel, with four 8.2-inch and fourteen 6-inch guns, and with heavy deck and turret armour plating. She was, however, relatively slow, with a maximum speed of 20.7 knots. She would be more than a match for *Leipzig*, but could not force an action if the German captain used his superior speed to avoid one.

Newcastle was one of the Royal Navy's most modern light cruisers, armed with two 6-inch and ten 4-inch guns, lightly armoured, and with a top speed of 26 knots. She could catch *Leipzig* and probably beat her in a duel; certainly the German ship would incur unacceptable damage.

The submarine workups, the arrival of *Idzumo* and *Newcastle*, and even *Rainbow*'s new ammunition outfit had transformed the naval situation. As long as the German force in the area consisted of only one or even two light cruisers any attempt at ransom under threat of bombardment would be too risky. There was now much less reason for the perhaps excessively fearful reaction of the British Columbia citizenry at the outbreak of war.

But back on August 8, when much was still in doubt, Admiral Kingsmill had written to General Gwatkin:

> *It is quite possible that the two German cruisers*
> *on that coast will force* Rainbow *to an action, and*
> *so disable her that the City of Vancouver will be*
> *open to attack, in which case they will no doubt*
> *demand a large ransom in coal, etc.*

Acting on this information the same day an alarmed Gwatkin ordered Military District 11 to ". . . be ready at a moment's notice to mobilize all troops on the coast to guard every coal dock." These purely precautionary measures led to overreaction and politicization of what should have been strictly military measures.

Perhaps inspired by the success of his submarine coup,

Premier McBride turned his attention to the order from Gwatkin just received by the district commander. Without consulting Ottawa, he convened a meeting of Lieutenant-Colonel Roy, the local commanding officers, and the Senior Naval Officer. Roy was unable to resist the premier's pressure. On August 10 he exceeded his orders by directing the immediate mobilization of all the Victoria units plus the entire 23rd Infantry Brigade at Vancouver. Including the already-mobilized garrison at Esquimalt, more than four thousand militiamen men were now on active service in British Columbia. Detachments were sent to Nanaimo and Prince Rupert and to guard railway bridges against sabotage, but the majority of the troops not at Esquimalt were retained in the Vancouver area.

Artillery being the most urgent requirement, Militia Headquarters railed the Coburg Heavy Battery from Quebec City to the west coast. On August 12 the people of Vancouver were encouraged by the sight of two of its four 60-pounder field guns being emplaced at Point Grey. The other two went to Victoria, where they became Vancouver Island's mobile reserve.

At the behest of the premier, the navy also added to Vancouver's artillery resources. Two spare 4-inch naval guns were rushed from Esquimalt to Stanley Park, where they were mounted in extemporized but solid emplacements under the supervision of a former Royal Navy gunnery officer. Amazingly, he was able to train the raw recruits of the Vancouver Volunteer Reserve unit so well and so quickly that by August 14 the two guns were operational.

Militia Headquarters was by no means convinced that large-scale mobilization in British Columbia was justified on military grounds, whatever the local political imperatives. By this time Ottawa must have felt that Premier McBride, and not Lieutenant-Colonel Roy, was the actual commander of Military District 11, and indeed of all forces on the west

HMCS Rainbow *at Prince Rupert, responding to a report of enemy cruisers in the area.*

coast. A trouble-shooter was needed. The choice fell on Major L.J. Lipsett, a seconded British officer on the staff of Military District 10 in Winnipeg. In mid-August he was dispatched to Victoria to become General Staff Officer to Roy and, above all, to make an objective threat assessment. The outcome of his mission will be described in Chapter Seven.

Coast Defences 1893 - 1938

N ▶

Rodd Hill
– Three 6-inch B.L. Guns
– Two 12-Pounder Q.F. Guns
– Two Defence Electric Lights

Submarine Mine Field
– 1983 - 1906

Duntze Head
– Two 12-Pounder Q.F. Guns

Black Rock
– Two 12-Pounder Q.F. Guns
– Two Defence Electric Lights

Macaulay Point
– Three 6-inch B.L. Guns

Work Point
– Garrison H.Q.

ESQUIMALT HARBOUR

Signal Hill
– Two 9.2-inch B.L. Guns

ESQUIMALT

VICTORIA HARBOUR

VICTORIA

Juan de Fuca Strait

Esquimalt defences, 1878–1938. Showing developments over the years and the situation in 1914.

NOTE
Esquimalt Coastal Defences

Thanks to geography, an enemy attempting to enter Halifax harbour would have to traverse a long and narrow entrance channel with batteries on both sides. Esquimalt did not possess this advantage, so its fortifications were necessarily disposed at right-angles to the enemy's line of approach.

The counter-bombardment battery of two 9.2-inch weapons was atop Signal Hill, near the dockyard entrance, covering a wide arc with excellent visibility. One fire-command post and fortress headquarters were also located here.

There were three intermediate range batteries. The Macaulay Point Battery mounted three 6-inch guns, as did the Fort Rodd position, with two in its Lower Battery and one in the Upper. A second fire command post was also located at Fort Rodd. Unlike at Halifax, the 6-inch guns at Esquimalt were of the outdated disappearing model, which meant that they had a slower rate of fire.

Three 12-pounder batteries each of two guns were assigned to the anti–torpedo boat task. On the eastern shore the examination battery at Black Rock was on continuous alert. A short distance to its north was the Duntze Head Battery, pointing west across the narrowest part of the entrance. Its counterpart opposite was the Belmont Battery, sited just south of the Fort Rodd Lower Battery. Two searchlights were located at Fort Rodd and two on the opposite side adjacent to Black Rock, capable of thoroughly illuminating the narrow channel to the dockyard. Each searchlight position had its own heavily protected generating room.

The batteries at Rodd Hill and Macaulay Point were vulnerable to attack by enemy landing parties approaching from the rear. They were therefore protected against assaults from that direction by concrete walls, loop-holed for rifles and machine guns. There was also a mobile company of garrison artillery, equipped with

13-pounder field guns and Maxim machine guns, to seek out and destroy the intruders before they reached the forts.

Overall control was exercised by fire command posts at Fort Rodd and Signal Hill. Garrison headquarters was also located in the latter position. A more detailed description of standard coastal defence weapons and control in the Esquimalt scenario will be found in the Appendix.

CHAPTER SEVEN
Consolidation,
September to December 1914

The events of August 1914 were so numerous that we have had to tell them in separate chapters for Halifax and Victoria. Through the remainder of the year the pace gradually slackened, and the tale can be followed in a single chapter, although not always in strict chronological order.

Beginning in September the real threat level declined, although the perceived level sometimes did not. At the same time the sea and land resources of the defences increased, and the soldiers and sailors of the fortresses and ships gained in experience and effectiveness. Unexpected problems continued to arise, but standard procedures gradually replaced ad hoc decision-making. In the beginning, the fortress cities had been uniquely menaced, but for them the war was now becoming more routine and less dangerous. Very shortly that would cease to be true for the country as a whole.

The local press in both Victoria and Halifax fully reported the events of August just described. But it was the news from Europe that captured most of the headlines and monopolized the attention of the public. Little wonder, since at times it appeared that the war might be lost in the first few weeks.

The German plan envisaged a great wheel through Belgium and northern France, the right flank passing west of Paris and swinging east to trap the bulk of the French army in its positions along the frontier. In the early stages all went well for the Germans, and the outnumbered allies were forced into a steady southward withdrawal. The papers were full of the stirring deeds of the French, the British Expeditionary Force, and the gallant Belgians, but the attentive reader could not help noticing that the reports were coming from locations closer and closer to the heart of France.

The Germans expected that the slow-moving Russians could be virtually ignored in the first few weeks, but the Russians were able to launch an invasion earlier than expected. Germany had to detach troops from the western front to help stem the Russians' advance. At the same time the German armies in France began to outrun their supplies. At the Battle of the Marne, from September 5–12, the allies pushed back and forced the Germans to withdraw to the north.

Each side now tried to outflank its opponent in what became a race to the sea. As their spearheads hurried north Allies and Germans left defending troops in opposing trenches that by the end of 1914 formed two parallel lines snaking from the Swiss border to the Channel coast just west of Ostend. Great battles with hitherto unimagined casualties would rage along this front for more than three years, but until 1918 gains and losses by either side would mostly be measured in yards rather than miles. The conflict became a war of attrition in which the Canadian Expeditionary Force would soon play its part.

By early September Rear-Admiral Cradock had decided that, whether armed or not, the German passenger liners were not going to sail from New York, and also that *Karlsruhe* and *Dresden* were operating independently and generally moving in a southerly direction. (Actually, *Karlsruhe* had sunk after an internal explosion, but this was not known for a very long time, and meanwhile her supposed presence continued to bedevil the strategic picture.) Thus, the enemy threat in the North Atlantic need no longer be considered serious. On the other hand it seemed likely to increase in South American waters, where the trade route to the United Kingdom was almost as important as the one from North America.

The Admiralty shared Cradock's opinion, and set up a new squadron under his command. In peacetime the Royal Navy did not have a South American Station, but since well before the war His Majesty's Ship *Glasgow* under Captain John Luce had been showing the flag and collecting intelligence in the area. Cradock set course for his new station in *Good Hope*, the Canadian midshipmen still aboard.

With the assignment of Admiral Cradock to the new southern theatre the North America and West Indies Station needed a replacement commander. As mentioned in Chapter Five, that officer was Rear-Admiral R. Phipps Hornby, then in command off Ireland. He arrived in Halifax on the former liner, now armed merchant cruiser, *Caronia* on September 14, shifting his flag temporarily to the battleship *Glory* on the nineteenth.

The convoy carrying the 1st Division of the Canadian Expeditionary Force was preparing to depart from Quebec City. At this point in the war there was as yet no submarine threat in the western Atlantic. To counter German surface raiders the close escort was to consist of five cruisers and one battleship, including *Glory* and *Niobe* from Phipps Hornby's squadron. As the convoy approached Britain it would be joined by a second battleship, while the whole of the Grand Fleet would be available in support. But detaching one of his cruisers would have left Phipps Hornby's remaining force woefully weak, and there were fears that *Niobe*'s propulsion system

SMS Dresden *in the Caribbean in August 1914.*
She evaded Admiral Cradock's Squadron and
later joined Admiral von Spee's Pacific force.

was unacceptably prone to breakdown. She was therefore held back, and the opportunity was lost for a Canadian ship to escort the first Canadian troops overseas.

On October 7 *Niobe* relieved *Suffolk* on the close-in patrol off New York, a duty she would perform in rotation for many months. At this time the troop convoy was en route to Britain, so vigilance was doubly necessary. On October 12 the *Ottawa Citizen* reported with pride:

If officers of an incoming merchantman that reached New York tonight are not mistaken one of the British warships now on guard off the harbor is the Canadian cruiser Niobe. *When she was outside the Ambrose Channel lightship at seven o'clock to night a warship suddenly threw her powerful searchlight across the* Vauban's *bow. Then with a Morse-light the warship ordered the merchantman to stop. A cutter promptly put off and pulled alongside the* Vauban. *The*

HMCS Niobe *in 1914, showing wartime appearance.*

*officer boarded her and after a conversation with
Captain Byrne allowed her to proceed.*

Canadians might indeed have taken pride in the activity of
their infant navy, but many must have wondered why *Niobe* was
stopping ships a few miles off the largest city and busiest port of
their southern neighbour, a neutral in the war now raging. In
fact the ship was participating in a British blockade of the key
American port of New York.

A blockade is a maritime strategy with a long history. Since
earliest times belligerents with superior naval strength had
blocked entry and exit from enemy ports as a means of apply-
ing pressure on their opponent. Of course an effective blockade
meant that enemy warships and merchant ships were prevented
from reaching the open ocean. But in time the strategy embraced
the idea of preventing the enemy from importing goods that
would assist him in carrying on the conflict.

The law of the sea had evolved the concept of contraband, which could be either unconditional or conditional. Unconditional contraband included arms, ammunition and other war material, plus goods capable of conversion to military purposes. Conditional contraband described purely civilian cargo, principally foodstuffs. However, if the blockading nation decided that the food was actually destined for the enemy's armed forces it could also be declared unconditional, and by 1914 any goods consigned to an enemy combatant were in practice regarded as contraband and therefore subject to seizure.

The law of the sea also demanded that a blockade must be declared, and that it must be made effective to be lawful.

Obviously, any merchant vessel belonging to the enemy was subject to sinking or capture without regard to its cargo. Thus, in practice the concept of contraband applied only to cargoes carried in neutral vessels. Any neutral merchant ship was subject to being stopped and searched by the navy of the blockading power. If her cargo was believed to be contraband a prize crew would be put aboard and the ship sent to a friendly port for adjudication by a prize court. Naturally, neutrals resented the practice.

As soon as war broke out Great Britain declared a blockade of Germany, later extended to Austria-Hungary and other German allies. For the Royal Navy blockade had a long history. Relentlessly applied for years against Napoleon, it had been a major contributor to his downfall. But as usual it had angered neutral nations, most notably inciting the United States to begin the War of 1812–1814. Once Napoleon had been overthrown the Royal Navy was free to impose a blockade of the United States' east coast, ruining its trade, and again becoming a major factor in bringing that war to an end.

Thanks to geography, it was easy for the Royal Navy to apply a close blockade in the North Sea and the entrance to the Baltic.

Neutral ships plying to and from continental ports stood a very good chance of being stopped and searched in these waters. In practice it was soon agreed that neutrals destined for continental Europe would call at British ports for examination and clearance. They would then be escorted through the British minefields.

But the blockade applied much more widely; neutrals sailing to Europe could be stopped anywhere in the Atlantic. At the beginning of the war the blockade mainly affected the merchant marines of the United States, Norway, and the Netherlands. American trade with Germany virtually ceased, and the American government remained under great pressure to retaliate against Britain. It would not be until 1917 that the United States entered the conflict on the allied side. By that time Germany had introduced unrestricted submarine warfare, which helped increase public support for the American government's decision to enter the war.

A blockade could be legally enforced anywhere outside the territorial waters of neutral nations, at that time a distance of three nautical miles to seaward of the high-water mark. In the autumn of 1914 several factors contributed to the British decision to enforce it in international waters — within sight of the city of New York.

We have already noted that significant numbers of German and Austrian reservists living in North America were recalled to their native countries on mobilization. Many converged on New York, in peacetime the principal port of embarkation for Europe. It was important for Britain to try to prevent them from reaching home. If discovered aboard a neutral vessel they were treated as prisoners of war and interned at Halifax or Bermuda. Not unnaturally there were vehement protests, and in October 1914 the removal of reservists from neutral ships off New York was suspended. The close blockade in European waters of course continued.

New York was also unique in harbouring thirty-eight German merchant ships, trapped there at the outbreak of war. Many were simple merchant steamers, nevertheless capable of acting as colliers and supply ships for the raiding cruisers operating in the western Atlantic. A potentially higher risk was posed by four crack passenger liners. Thanks to their high speed these vessels would be very dangerous commerce raiders if they could be armed and reach the open sea. Before the war it had been rumoured that some of them actually carried guns and ammunition in their holds, and that a portion of their crews were naval reservists.

The *Kronprinzessin Cecilie* had actually sailed for Europe on August 1, carrying passengers and gold bullion. On August 4 she was within a day or two of Hamburg, but certain to be intercepted in the heavily patrolled North Sea. To prevent the gold she was carrying from falling into British hands she was ordered to seek shelter in a neutral port. Reversing course, she steamed for Boston, having disguised herself as the White Star liner *Olympic*. She was interned there until the Americans entered the war in 1917, when she became a troopship.

The story of the escape of the liner *Kronprinz Wilhelm* and her subsequent arming by *Karlsruhe* has already been told in Chapter Five. She became a successful raider until forced to intern herself in the United States when supplies and coal could no longer be obtained. The converted-liner threat was very real.

All vessels leaving or entering New York harbour were stopped and boarded by Royal Navy personnel, their captains questioned, and their manifests examined for contraband and suspicious individuals. It was very desirable to intercept ships as close to the port entrance as possible, before they dispersed into the broad Atlantic. With the fast liners it was critical to do so; once in open waters their speed would allow them to vanish until they chose to reappear, possibly armed and dangerous. Of course in 1914 radar lay more than thirty years in the future. As in Nelson's time the only means of detection by day or night was the human eye.

The United States protested to the British government that the cruisers were patrolling too close inshore. *Charybdis* in particular was alleged to have crossed the three-mile line. Phipps Hornby denied that his ships had ever entered American territorial waters. However, in early October he did establish a more distant five-nautical-mile patrol boundary to allow for navigational error, increased to six miles just before Christmas. The captain of one of his ships could disregard these limits when in hot pursuit of a suspicious vessel, as long as he remained outside territorial waters.

Relations with the United States Navy were good; sometimes the Americans passed useful information to the British–Canadian patrols. Anxious to preserve a strict neutrality the authorities at New York intended to hold any ships detected in fitting out for war. In addition, belligerent vessels were warned not to sail without notice to naval authorities, to include their cargo and passenger manifests.

The only ships available for the patrol were *Charybdis*, *Glory*, *Suffolk*, *Lancaster*, and *Niobe*, plus the armed merchant cruiser *Caronia*. At any given time at least one of these was likely to be under repair at Halifax or Bermuda. On each rotation a ship spent sixteen days on the station, regardless of weather. In winter, temperatures would fall many degrees below zero, the spray freezing in a solid coating all over the ship, making it almost impossible to work the guns. Halifax rather than Bermuda had been chosen as the blockade support base because of its proximity to the trade routes, ease of access by day or night, and better wireless communications. A wireless station was set up at Cape Sable, and chartered vessels sixty miles off Cape Cod acted as relays to keep the ships in touch with Halifax.

Two or three ships were required on station off New York at all times, patrolling sectors delimited by bearings from the

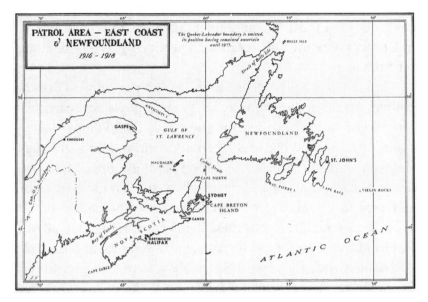

East coast patrol areas, 1916–1918.

Ambrose Light Vessel. Allowance for the 650 nautical mile passage to and from Halifax had to be built into the schedule. After coaling, storing and necessary maintenance there was little or no opportunity for crew rest before the next patrol. As the strain on the ships' companies increased and winter weather set in many must have much regretted that Bermuda was not their chosen base. The shortage of ships meant that New York was the only American port that could be watched, although it was known that German merchant vessels, including fast liners, were at Boston and other places.

By mid-1915 the patrol had captured one German armed merchant cruiser and three naval auxiliaries, and put prize crews aboard seven Norwegian and American ships for transit to a friendly port for adjudication. On January 2, 1915, *Niobe* boarded the SS *Brookby*, bound for Bari, Italy. That country remained neutral, although bound by a prewar alliance with Germany. *Brookby* carried a cargo of wheat, and it was suspected that it was actually destined for Germany. A prize crew was therefore put aboard and the ship sent to Gibraltar for adjudication.

False reports continued to be a source of distraction and a waste of resources. After her first patrol *Niobe* was back in Halifax on October 22, in urgent need of repairs to her steam condensers. But the very next day a suspicious three-funneled cruiser was reported in the Strait of Belle Isle, sighted by a Norwegian ship and by observers on Anticosti Island. *Niobe* left at once to investigate. After a fruitless search of the coasts of Anticosti and western Newfoundland she returned to home port for a complete re-tubing of her unreliable condensers.

In his report of proceedings for 1914 Phipps Hornby had much to say about the support rendered to his squadron by the Halifax base and other facilities.

At the precautionary stage the Halifax naval intelligence centre had been stood up under *Niobe*'s navigating officer. It was not transferred to Admiralty control on the outbreak of war, but by default it became a source of intelligence for the Royal Navy commanders in the area, first Rear-Admiral Cradock and later Rear-Admiral Phipps Hornby. Given the very British orientation of Royal Canadian Navy officers it was not surprising that the centre sometimes acted as though its primary responsibility was to the senior Royal Navy officer afloat, and not to Naval Service Headquarters, much to the displeasure of the Ottawa authorities.

Halifax would in fact have been the best location for the Royal Navy's own Western Atlantic intelligence centre. Unfortunately the Admiralty insisted on establishing it in St. John's, Newfoundland, despite Phipps Hornby's strong representations to the contrary. In 1914 the dual processes led to confusion and friction as Canada persisted in asserting its national interest in the vital realm of intelligence. Co-operative arrangements were worked out, and on leaving the station Phipps Hornby commended the officer in charge, Acting-Commander Charles White, for the support he had received.

Security was always a matter of concern. Censorship of transatlantic cable messages was effective, but inland telegraph traffic was not monitored, so leakage to the United States was always possible. A need-to-know policy was implemented, but the Halifax press was allowed to report warships' movements, and the cap tallies of sailors ashore continued to show the name of their ships. There seems to be no evidence that any operation was ever compromised, but it is scarcely credible that the authorities allowed such elementary breaches of security to continue.

Given the underfunding of the dockyard after its 1906 transfer to Canada it is hardly surprising that the facilities were not found adequate under wartime conditions. Only one alongside berth was suitable for large vessels, so coaling usually had to be carried out from colliers, a much longer process when time was often of the essence. Much use had to be made of the commercial resources of the Halifax Graving Dock Company. That firm was supposed to give priority to naval requirements, but apparently did not always do so. After her grounding *Niobe* had been repaired in the drydock. But larger ships could not be accommodated, a matter of concern in the event of underwater damage to one of the battleships, battle cruisers, or large liners that frequently operated in the local area.

Phipps Hornby noted that "The supply of stores has been a continuing source of trouble." In Royal Navy parlance, there were two types of stores. Naval stores were mostly physical items of approved admiralty pattern necessary to the maintenance and habitability of a ship. These he found quite unobtainable locally, making his squadron dependent on regular shipments from stocks in the United Kingdom. That indispensable commodity, pusser's or navy-pattern rum, was also deemed to be a naval store. It may surprise many that this too was unobtainable in the port of Halifax.

As the name implies, victualling stores referred to food for the ship's companies. These were available in Halifax, "but acceptance must be made by a Royal Naval officer because political influence governs the award of contracts to a significant extent, and the local Stores Officers require support in rejecting consignments." Despite the problems, Phipps Hornby commended three of these Stores Officers.

The report was not entirely negative. Captain Corbett and Engineer Lieutenant-Commander John F. Bell merited favourable mention for the way in which the aged *Niobe* was brought into service and maintained thereafter. Shore barracks for transients were considered adequate, as were the medical arrangements in the dockyard sick quarters and the naval hospital, the latter located in the now unused immigration facilities on the city's waterfront.

Finally, Phipps Hornby expressed his gratitude to Rear-Admiral Kingsmill "for the assistance he has afforded me and the very hearty manner in which he has co-operated with me in every way, thus creating very cordial relationships between the two services." It is easy to believe that the new navy spared no effort in its support of its illustrious parent, perhaps unconsciously compensating for its inability to make its own significant operational contribution.

From a Canadian standpoint the main recommendation in the report was expressed as follows:

> *The war has brought the importance of*
> *Halifax as a naval base into prominence . . .*
> *the subject should be raised with the Dominion*
> *Authorities at the conclusion of hostilities, and if*
> *necessary arrangement made to provide the Yard*
> *with sufficient work during peace to enable it to*
> *maintain a state of preparedness for war.*

On November 17, 1914, the Secretary of State for the Colonies telegraphed a warning to the Governors General of Canada, Australia, and New Zealand, and the government of India for information and action by their ministers. Enclosed was an Admiralty memorandum on the subject of mine-laying, which the Germans were using extensively in home waters and which could also be initiated abroad.

The memorandum went on to state that, even though mine-layers were large ships, there could be no guarantee that they could not reach the open sea. They carried up to eight hundred mines that could be sown in waters up to six hundred feet in depth. Fields were usually placed on the continental shelf twenty to forty miles from shore, out of sight of land, to avoid detection and make sweeping more difficult.

The memorandum recommended that shipping leaving and approaching overseas ports should use new routes to avoid areas in which the mines would probably have been laid, and that other appropriate measures should be taken. At Halifax there were barely sufficient vessels to sweep the relatively shallow harbour itself, let alone critical zones out to the hundred-fathom line. Nevertheless, as 1914 drew to a close more civilian vessels were taken up for conversion, and patrols were instituted in the Bay of Fundy.

In 1915 J.K.L. Ross was bold enough to again risk American justice by procuring a second yacht for conversion, under much the same circumstances as when he bought *Tarantula* from Vanderbilt. Having obtained leave, he travelled to New York to purchase the yacht *Winchester* from Peter W. Rouss, at a cost of $100,000. He was reimbursed for his purchase expenses, but not for the refit of what became His Majesty's Canadian Ship *Grilse*, a 35-knot vessel armed with a 12-pounder gun and one torpedo tube.

The government had been aware even before the war that the German intelligence centre in New York would do whatever it could to damage the Canadian war effort. Its most ambitious plan was to gather a large force of German reservists and Irish nationalists to launch a full-scale invasion from American territory, the Fenian raids writ large. To give the men cover under international law, they were all to be dressed as cowboys to represent uniformed and authorized combatants!

Such fantasies could be easily dismissed, but other ideas were more practical. In September 1914 Captain von Papen, the German spy-master at New York, recruited men to sabotage the Welland Canal locks. The aim was to disrupt preparations for the dispatch of the Canadian Expeditionary Force to England. The Force sailed before the attempt could be made, and the plan was therefore called off.

After Japan entered the war on the allied side the Germans believed that large numbers of Japanese troops could be transported across the Pacific to Vancouver, railed to Halifax, and thence onward by ship to fight in France. The obvious countermeasure was to interrupt traffic by blowing bridges along the main lines. Quite apart from the Japanese threat, any interruption in rail traffic would adversely affect the movement of soldiers and materiel to Europe and indeed the whole Canadian economy. The target list included bridges across the Fraser River in British Columbia, and at Lac Mégantic, Debec, Fraserville, and Perth-Andover in eastern Canada. The latter group was identified by Major Franz von Papen, the military attaché at the German embassy in Washington.

A subsidiary of the Canadian Pacific Railroad operated a line from Quebec through Maine to Saint John and Halifax. It crossed the St. Croix River on a bridge between Vanceboro, Maine, and St. Croix, New Brunswick. In New York, von Papen made contact with Werner Horn, an army reserve lieutenant who had been recalled to Germany but was unable to find transport because of the blockade. Out of patriotism he undertook to blow the bridge, for which feat he was also to be paid $700. Carrying a suitcase full of dynamite he travelled by rail to Vanceboro, where he checked into a hotel. His behaviour aroused suspicion, but he was able to convince an American immigration inspector that he was on legitimate business.

On the night of February 1, 1915, he donned his German uniform and placed his explosives on the Canadian side of the bridge. Train traffic was heavy, and not wanting to kill anyone he had to wait a considerable time before a quiet period allowed him to light the fuse and return to the United States, just as his device exploded. Windows were blown out on both sides of the border, but the bridge was not extensively damaged and the line returned to full operation within a few days.

In the United States he served eighteen months for unlawful transport of dangerous goods, before being extradited to Canada where he was sentenced to ten years in Dorchester Penitentiary. In 1921 he was judged insane and returned to Germany.

In October 1914 the government began to raise the 2nd Division of the CEF. One of the units authorized was the 25th Infantry Battalion, which began recruiting and training at the Halifax armouries and on the commons. This was Nova Scotia's first attempt to directly provide a battalion for overseas service, and the vast majority of the men were from the province. It was at full strength by December, with a 10 per cent reserve. The Halifax Rifles did provide a draft of fifty-two all ranks to the 25th, but one can imagine the feelings of the rest of the men of the 63rd and 66th Regiments, still tied to fortress defence, watching the 25th prepare for a service they would have given anything to undertake themselves.

***

We saw that in mid-August Major Lipsett had been sent to British Columbia to render an objective report on the necessity for what the Ottawa authorities saw as the excessive strength of mobilized militia in the province. At the time allied naval reinforcements had yet to arrive, but both submarines were minimally operational and patrolling the Strait of Juan de Fuca turn and turnabout. Obsolescent as she was *Rainbow* at least had proper ammunition for her outdated main armament. Lipsett considered this force alone was a sufficient deterrent to a German attack. Vancouver and Nanaimo were not in his view severely threatened.

Apart from the Esquimalt garrison and a detachment at Prince Rupert, he considered that the hastily mobilized militia infantry units could safely be given a reduced role, providing vital point guards while generating detachments for overseas service. A large portion of their mobilized strength could then be stood down, with significant financial savings.

In keeping with political realities in British Columbia, Lipsett's conclusions were submitted to Premier McBride, who accepted them. At Militia Headquarters General Gwatkin in turn advised Minister Hughes that the plan should be implemented.

A considerable delay ensued, during which *Idzumo* and *Newcastle* arrived, further strengthening Lipsett's case. At length the minister agreed, and on September 10 Gwatkin directed Lieutenant-Colonel Roy to implement the reduction.

In the interim the premier's views had changed. On September 12 Gwatkin received the following from Roy:

> *By request of Premier BC a conference was*
> *held at which local federal members, commanding*
> *officers, and Col Stuart (commanding 23rd*
> *Infantry Brigade) were threatened, with result men*
> *volunteering for overseas will remain mobilized.*

In effect, for political reasons a premier had assumed command of the national militia within his own province. Hughes was absent from Ottawa, so Gwatkin passed this astonishing communication to Prime Minister Borden, who was temporarily acting as minister of militia. Borden's compromise was to confirm the implementation of the Lipsett plan, but to caution Roy that "when in doubt you are to seek the advice of Sir Richard McBride."

As Roger Sarty has observed, the situation was truly bizarre. The 30th Regiment British Columbia Horse had no conceivable role. However, it successfully refused to demobilize or even to serve dismounted, thanks to the support of federal Minister of Agriculture Burrell, who had been one of the premier's confidants in the submarine affair. Despite such examples, the quietly persistent Roy did succeed in reducing 23rd Infantry Brigade strength from 2,037 in mid-September to 1,092 on October 3.

Several factors unique to B.C. contributed to the unprecedented political–military imbroglio. Partial demobilization at Vancouver while the Esquimalt garrison remained at full strength revived memories of the old Mainland versus Island rivalry. Militia commanders hated to see their units run down, and being men of considerable influence, did not hesitate to complain through political channels. The most serious concern was the Vancouver unemployment situation, which had not improved with the outbreak of war. Mobilization had brought some relief. But it also attracted large numbers of British subjects who flocked to Vancouver to enlist, not only from the province but from the Pacific islands and northwestern America from Alaska to Mexico. Partial demobilization added a thousand men to the number of the city's welfare recipients.

When *Newcastle* reached Esquimalt her commanding officer, Captain F.A. Powlett, Royal Navy, became the senior naval officer afloat on the west coast, responsible to the Admiralty for operational control of *Idzumo*, *Rainbow*, and the two submarines, as well as his own ship. To conceal their movements *Newcastle* and *Idzumo* operated from Barkley Sound on the west coast of Vancouver Island. When the force was at sea *Rainbow* patrolled the entrance to the Juan de Fuca Strait, while *Idzumo* took station off San Francisco. In *Newcastle*, Powlett twice ranged further south along the coast, but never overtook *Leipzig*.

Powlett was not slow to fill what he saw as a vacuum by stretching his mandate to include the Esquimalt dockyard and other shore resources, notwithstanding the fact that constitutionally they remained under Canadian control. He must have been made aware of the latest intelligence on von Spee's whereabouts, but, like the politicians, chose to act as though the powerful German squadron posed an immediate threat to British Columbia.

Von Spee intended to make for South America, but even with advance planning it would take some time for German representatives there to charter colliers to replenish his bunkers. In the meantime he decided to damage allied interests in the central Pacific. At the very beginning of the war an expedition from New Zealand had captured Apia, the capital of German Samoa. Von Spee lacked the resources to retake the place, but he hoped that a surprise arrival would trap some military shipping. At dawn on September 14 his squadron appeared off the harbour. No ships were there, so he sailed away. When last seen by the New Zealanders he was steering to the west, away from South America. That information was passed to the Admiralty, which was completely fooled by von Spee's elementary ruse, and wrongly deduced that his next objective was Fiji or perhaps even New Zealand.

Those arguing for comprehensive mobilization received further ammunition in September with von Spee's sudden and unexpected reappearance. Having vanished after his abortive attack on Apia, the German admiral arrived off the French island of Tahiti on September 22, outside the capital town, Papeete. Stored there were 5,000 tons of best quality steaming coal that

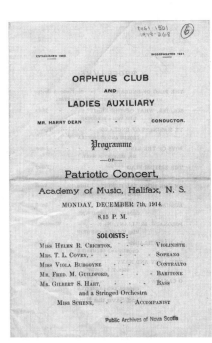

Public Archives of Nova Scotia

*First page of programme for Halifax
Patriotic Concert, winter 1914. The
attachment to the Empire is very evident.*

the admiral hoped the French would give up to avoid bombardment. This action again underlines the main logistic problem facing the East Asiatic Squadron: the need to coal. In desperation, the defenders set fire to the stocks. Balked in his intentions, von Spee contented himself with sinking a lone French gunboat before vanishing over the horizon.

***

When news of Papeete reached British Columbia the spectre again arose of the entire enemy squadron off Vancouver, Prince Rupert, or Nanaimo, guns trained on the shore, demanding supplies and money. Von Spee had already made up his mind to make for South America, but that intention was unknown to the allies, who regarded it as just one of several courses of action still open to him.

The provincial reaction was well summed up by two telegrams from the censor in Victoria to Ottawa:

*Apprehension attack general. Local hotel
men say California and Washington hotel men
divert tourist travel saying dangerous to come to
Victoria. Excitement fostered by attitude local
militia and politicians. Act and talk as if German*

fleet in Straits. Roy except. He cool, but baited by
offices and politicians whose aid officers enlist.
MP Barnard and McBride told me they consider
Roy absurdly economical.

And a few days later:

September 27th I had confidential chat
Roy . . . He was desirous demobilization.
Unemployment as one of arguments against
demobilization frankly and extensively used.
Complete demobilization until German ships
accounted for would unquestionably produce
universal pain increase popular anxiety. Partial
demobilization if politicians allay anxiety
instead of fomenting it practicable.

Such measured views could not compete with politics. After consulting with the Prime Minister, General Gwatkin conceded defeat. Depending on the employment situation up to 2,500 men would be kept on active service. Something was salvaged by insisting that all must be physically fit and must be volunteers for overseas service. By November 1914 the number of active militiamen in the province had crept up to more than 2,900. Gwatkin wrote the Deputy Minister of Militia, Major-General Eugène Fiset, that "In my opinion the number of men under arms is in excess of military requirements . . . but as I believe it would be worse than useless to advocate any reduction I propose to hold my peace." Fiset contented himself with the reply, "I quite agree."

All this was allowed to unfold despite the fact that von Spee's true intentions should have become obvious. After leaving Papeete he sailed to the Marquesas Islands, arriving on

September 26. Here he coaled and replenished food and water. Unexpectedly, von Spee's wireless operators made contact with the light cruiser *Dresden*. Never part of his command, she had been in the Caribbean but was gradually proceeding south on the east coast of South America, preying on the important trade routes.

✳✳✳

On October 4 von Spee sent a wireless message to *Dresden* and *Leipzig*, directing them to join him at Easter Island. Perhaps because *Dresden* had different code books than the Pacific squadron the message was sent in the clear, and was intercepted by the British station at Suva, Fiji. Easter Island was a well-chosen rendezvous if von Spee's objective was Chile, but made little sense if the united and reinforced East Asiatic Squadron was bound for British Columbia. Nevertheless the possibility could not be ignored that this was just another of von Spee's ruses.

Again the premier became involved, this time on the naval side of the west-coast defence problem. Without informing Ottawa, he initiated discussions with Powlett and Hose. The undefended Seymour Narrows between the mainland and the north end of Vancouver Island offered von Spee an unlikely but possible means of bypassing Powlett's Esquimalt-based forces and threatening Nanaimo and Vancouver via the Georgia Strait. Naval Service Headquarters was informed that the ad hoc group had decided to mine the narrows and erect a protective battery. Roy actually prepared to remobilize the mainland militia, but Gwatkin ordered him not to do so, and to try instead to prevent panic.

Sixteen controlled mines were available in the magazine at Esquimalt, where they had been stored after the submarine mining unit was dissolved. Canadian Government Ship *Newington* prepared to lay them across the entrance to the narrows in case of need, and in the meantime the passage was partially obstructed with materials obtained locally. Two spare 4-inch naval guns from *Shearwater* manned by naval reserve personnel formed the supporting battery, and a local fish packing company provided three fifty-foot motorboats armed with torpedoes to patrol the eastern exit from the narrows. Since Powlett had naval operational control he had not exceeded his authority so far, but certainly did so when he ordered a local militia unit to take over manning of the battery.

Ottawa was understandably concerned at the west-coast habit of presenting it with *faits accomplis*, along with the accompanying bills. In October Naval Service Headquarters appointed former Royal Navy Rear-Admiral W.O. Storey, retired in Guelph, Ontario, to be Senior Naval Officer at Esquimalt. His instructions conveyed a clear message:

> *It is pointed out that this appointment does not*
> *permit of a flag being flown, nor does it give you*
> *any authority over the movements of HM or HMC*
> *ships. It is intended that this appointment should*
> *be purely an administrative one and you should act*
> *in an advisory capacity in questions arising as to*
> *the defence of the coast of British Columbia. Your*
> *dealings with the senior imperial service officer on*
> *the coast will require to be handled with great tact.*

Storey's experience and judgement brought a more regular and balanced approach to the west-coast defence scene. Having been promoted to Vice-Admiral on the retired list, Storey would later assume the Senior Naval Officer's duties at Halifax in 1918. Again, this was in response to the tendency of senior British officers there to exceed their authority in Canadian matters. The previous incumbent, Captain Martin, was rumoured to be too ready to accommodate such efforts, and was transferred to take Storey's place as Senior Naval Officer at Esquimalt.

Meantime Rear-Admiral Sir Christopher Cradock had been guarding the South American trade routes while trying to track down the elusive *Dresden* and *Karlsruhe*; he was still unaware that the latter ship had self-destructed. In addition to his flagship *Good Hope* his motley squadron included the obsolescent protected cruiser *Monmouth*, the modern light cruiser *Glasgow*, and the armed merchant cruiser *Otranto*. The latter ship had almost no combat value, and was thus useless except to extend Cradock's search line by fifteen miles. In mid-September Victor Hatheway wrote to a sister in Fredericton that, "We are hot on the trail of the enemy ships," i.e., *Dresden* and (supposedly) *Karlsruhe*. Obviously, his morale was high, and von Spee's squadron had yet to become the object of Cradock's quest. But with the intercepted information that the German squadron had been ordered to Easter Island Cradock's mission changed dramatically. He received orders from the Admiralty to guard the trade routes on the west coast of South America and to eliminate the East Asiatic Squadron. To render his force strong enough to do so the modern armoured cruiser *Defence* and the old battleship *Canopus* were ordered to join him.

On October 22, the 109th anniversary of the Battle of Trafalgar, *Good Hope* was at Port Stanley in the Falkland Islands. It was forbidden to give away the ship's location in letters home, but Midshipman William Palmer managed to evade the order by buying a local illustrated postcard and sending it by ordinary mail rather than through the censored official route. At this time *Canopus* joined Cradock, but reported that her speed could not exceed twelve knots because of condenser problems. The Admiralty by now had diverted *Defence* to other duties but neglected to inform Cradock.

The admiral was faced with a dilemma. He could hope to engage

Rear-Admiral Storey was appointed to the post of Senior Naval Officer Esquimalt to maintain Canadian rights against overzealous Royal Navy officers.

the German squadron successfully when in company with the heavily armoured *Canopus* and her four 12-inch guns. But he could never catch von Spee if his own squadron's maximum speed was limited to that of the old battleship.

Nevertheless he passed through the Strait of Magellan and on October 26 concentrated his squadron at Vallenar, a deserted anchorage on the Chilean coast. Here the ships coaled from colliers while waiting for *Canopus*; on the same day von Spee was coaling at the island of Más Afuera. Both British and Germans were disregarding Chile's neutrality by flagrantly using her territorial waters. The Canadian midshipmen had leave to ramble on the heavily forested coast, and returned on board soaked after a tumble into a jungle stream.

The opposing squadrons were now about 2,400 kilometres of each other, and converging on Valparaiso. Neither knew exactly where his opponent was, but each had measured the other's strength. A battle was still not inevitable, but the odds against an encounter were rapidly narrowing. Cradock and von Spee had met and become friends before the war, when there was much sympathy between the officers of the two navies. Both may well have reflected on the fate that had brought them to this rendezvous.

Cradock was outside the coverage of the Falkland's wireless

Map illustrating the movements of the British and German squadrons leading to the Battle of Coronel and the later Battle of the Falkland Islands.

station, so on October 27 he dispatched *Glasgow* on ahead to the Chilean port of Coronel to collect his cabled messages and mail from the British consul. The next day he followed with the rest of the squadron, except *Canopus*, which again needed to carry out repairs. Von Spee had left Más Afuera the day before.

After touching at Coronel, on the morning of November 1 *Glasgow* rendezvoused with the other ships northwest of that port. A near gale was raging, but the sun shone brightly. Cradock set up a search line with his ships fifteen miles apart and steamed north. At 4 p.m. *Glasgow* sighted and identified the German squadron to the northeast, steering south. Cradock formed his line of battle in the order *Good Hope, Monmouth, Glasgow,* and *Otranto,* also on a southerly course, and with his squadron to the west of the German.

By an accident of geography the British ships were keeping the same local time as the Maritime provinces; the families of the four Canadian midshipmen would be sitting down to their Sunday dinners as the opposing squadrons went to action stations.

Sunset was at 6:30 p.m. Cradock's only hope was to engage just before that time, when the setting sun would blind the

Completely outclassed in her gunnery duel with Scharnhorst, Good Hope *took fire and disapppeared in a huge explosion. There were no survivors.*

German gunners. He turned toward them to narrow the range, but von Spee frustrated the manoeuvre with his superior speed. Exactly at sunset the Germans closed the range and engaged the British ships, now silhouetted against the afterglow.

The outcome was never in doubt. Cradock detached the lightly armed *Otranto* before the action began. Early in the battle the crippled *Monmouth* fell out of the line and was later sunk by *Nürnberg*. While the British could only aim at the enemy gun flashes, the German ships were firing four salvos a minute at the clearly visible *Good Hope*, now enveloped in flames. At 7:50 an 8.2-inch shell struck her between the mainmast and the after funnel, followed almost immediately by a terrific explosion that flung flame and debris more than two hundred feet into the air. One of her after 6-inch guns fired twice more, and then she fell silent. As the heavy British cruisers were put out of action *Glasgow* escaped to warn *Canopus*.

ROLL OF HONOR, CANADIAN NAVAL SERVICE—Passed with H.M.S. Good Hope in Southern Seas, while fighting for the Empire, (No. 1) Midshipman Silver, Halifax, N.S.; (No. 2) Midshipman Palmer, Halifax, N.S.; (No. 3) Midshipman Cann, Yarmouth, N.S.; (No. 4) Midshipman Hatheway, Fredericton, N.B.

The four midshipmen lost at Coronel were the first Canadian casualties of the Great War. Here their loss is commemorated in the Montreal Star.

***

No one in the German ships had actually seen the flagship go down. Thus, von Spee did not immediately realize the magnitude of his success. Conceivably, *Good Hope* had remained afloat and escaped in the darkness or perhaps had beached herself on the coast. Joined by Chilean warships, the Germans searched for two days, but not a trace was ever found of the flagship, the admiral, nine hundred men, or the Royal Canadian Navy's first casualties, who were indeed the country's first casualties of the war.

On November 5 the Halifax *Herald* reported rumours of a battle off the coast of Chile, which the Admiralty was unable to confirm. The next issue acknowledged that there had indeed been a battle, but reported with certainty that *Good Hope* had not taken part. It was not until November 7 that the paper printed the true story, under the headline: **We will never forget our four brave boys.** On the inside pages there were pictures of Halifax natives William Palmer and Arthur Silver, and also of *Good Hope* and *Monmouth*. The paper noted:

> As H.M.S. Good Hope *was at Halifax early in the war her loss causes particular sorrow here. When this cruiser steamed up Halifax harbour on August 14 her crew lined the deck and with the ship's band playing patriotic airs she was the object of interest to those on the waterfront.*

After Coronel both coasts seemed vulnerable to the threat posed by the East Asiatic Squadron. One of von Spee's options was to turn north to operate on the west coast of the Americas or perhaps to pass through the Panama Canal to the Atlantic, although it was uncertain whether the Americans would permit the transit. A combined British-Japanese-Canadian blocking force led by the Australian battle cruiser *Australia* was concentrated off Mexico, and later proceeded to the Galapagos Islands. Although theoretically part of the force, *Rainbow* could not keep up, and mainly functioned as a wireless link with Esquimalt.

When there seemed to be a significant likelihood that von Spee would actually turn north Captain Hose signalled Naval Service

British battle cruisers were easily identified by their tripod masts. German Admiral von Spee unexpectedly encountered two of them at the Falkland Islands, and his squadron was virtually destroyed.

Headquarters, "Submit that Admiralty be asked to arrange with Senior Officer of allied squadron . . . that Canadian ship *Rainbow* shall if possible be in company when engaged with enemy." Ottawa turned down his request, one of the reasons given being ". . . if the *Rainbow* were lost, immediately there would be much criticism on account of her age in being sent to engage modern vessels." Since she had been ordered to do just that at the beginning of the war the rationale seems somewhat inconsistent.

At the special Colonial Conference of 1909 the Admiralty had recommended that the dominions should each acquire a "fleet unit" of one battle cruiser, two light cruisers, and six destroyers, to be built in the United Kingdom and to be partly manned by the Royal Navy until enough dominion sailors were trained. Australia had accepted the recommendation, and in 1914 possessed a viable force. As in Canada, its ships came under British operational control at the outbreak of war, and several distinguished themselves in both the Atlantic and Pacific oceans throughout the conflict. Of course, Canada had turned down the recommendation in favour of Laurier's plan for a Canadian-constructed squadron, with the results we know.

HMS Cornwall *undergoing repairs in Esquimalt for damages sustained at the Battle of the Falkland Islands, during which* Cornwall *sank* Leipzig.

There would be no further encounter in the Pacific. Now that the German squadron had eliminated Cradock's force there was apparently nothing to oppose an entry into the Atlantic via the Strait of Magellan. Von Spee decided to try to break through to Germany. Against the advice of his friend, the captain of *Gneisenau*, he also determined to attack undefended Port Stanley in the Falklands en route, with a view to obtaining coal for the passage.

Cradock's defeat caused consternation at the Admiralty. At 1 p.m. London time on November 4, Admiral Sir John Jellicoe, in command of the Grand Fleet, was ordered to detach the battle cruisers *Invincible* and *Inflexible* "for foreign service." They coaled and proceeded to Plymouth for rectification of defects. Churchill ordered the dockyard to disregard normal routine to ensure a quick turnaround. As an incentive, tradesmen were ordered to sail in the ships should any defects remain.

With eight 12-inch guns each, and a speed of 25.5 knots, the battle cruisers were infinitely superior to von Spee's armoured cruisers, which they could both outrun and outfight. A number of armoured and light cruisers were added to the force, under the command of Vice-Admiral Sir Doveton Sturdee, who had in part been responsible for the dispositions that had placed Cradock in an impossible position.

Although the force coaled twice on its passage south the secret had been well kept. On the evening of December 5 Sturdee's squadron anchored at Port Stanley, to the complete surprise of the governor. At dawn the next day von Spee's squadron appeared off the town; to his astonishment the harbour was crowded with warships. When their distinctive tripod masts confirmed the presence of battle cruisers he knew his doom was sealed, just as Cradock must have known before Coronel. Again the result was preordained. By sunset all the German ships but one were at the bottom, and von Spee and his sons were dead. *Dresden* alone survived, but she was tracked down and sunk within weeks.

CHAPTER EIGHT
Afterwards

Reference has already been made to the disappointment and even anger felt by those members of the two garrisons who fervently wished to proceed overseas, but who were not allowed to do so because of their fortress duties.

As early as 1915 a letter appeared in the Halifax *Herald* protesting the government's failure to recruit for 1 Royal Canadian Garrison Artillery to release men for overseas. Signed "Gunner," it pleaded, "After being in the outforts since the war began, and the prospect of another dreary year or more, I think it is time we had a change."

During the war many of the men condemned to home service attempted to stow away on troop transports, and some actually made it to France. When the 1st Division was being organized Captain G.M. Brew of the of the militia artillery led a draft from the regiment to Camp Valcartier. When told that he himself was not needed he resigned his commission, took ship to England, and served with the Royal Artillery for the rest of the war.

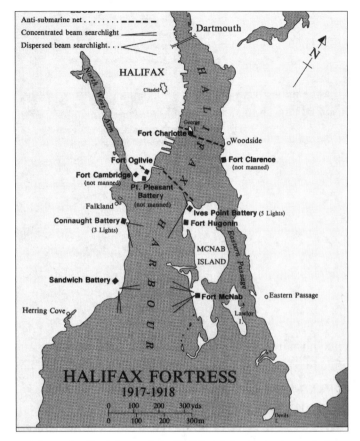

This map shows the final form of the Halifax defences at the end of WWI.
Neither the submarine nets nor Connaught Battery were in existence in 1914.

Since neither the regular nor militia artillery units were up to strength it was with great difficulty that all the batteries continued to be manned at minimum levels. The duty was arduous. All guns were kept loaded.

> *Night and day, all through the war . . . men*
> *to work the guns had to be near them and alert,*
> *while at each gun was a sentry, who was relieved*
> *every hour, and who was to watch to seaward*

*for the approach of any hostile craft, not a very
arduous task at first sight, but enough to make
most want to be overseas after a few months of it.*

The general belief that living conditions in the fortress were
better than in France was not always justified, thanks in part to
the Halifax climate.

*The casemates in which the men were supposed
to be quartered . . . were unfit for occupation as,
owing to long disuse, they were in a very damp and
unsanitary condition. The unit (regular garrison
artillery) was therefore placed under canvas, and it
was late in December before any attempt was made
to provide proper and suitable winter quarters.
Owing to a fine distinction being made between the
Militia and Overseas forces, which only an army
man can understand, the men were not provided
with a full kit, even boots being denied them until
many were actually barefoot. Underclothing and
other necessities had to be purchased by the men
themselves, until at last the responsible authorities
awakened to the fact that there was a real war on.*

*They had however the consolation that they
were doing a necessary and valuable work and
were buoyed up by the hope that their chance
would yet come; and if not, the State would at
least recognize their volunteer service as at least
equal to those, many of whom were draftees,
who had not proceeded further than England or
St. Lucia.*

It was not to be. For many of the volunteers their worst fears were realized. After four years of frustrating and demanding service they were left without recognition or medals, forgotten amid the enthusiastic welcome and permanent remembrance accorded to those who had left Canada.

Although shame was felt on both coasts it is much more evident in the records of the Halifax units. For very good reasons the proportion of men released from the Esquimalt garrison seems to have been considerably higher than in Halifax.

We have seen that British naval pressure was habitually applied to maintain and even improve fortresses that protected important naval bases. After von Spee's destruction the Esquimalt base lost much of its strategic importance from the Royal Navy's point of view, and its defences could be virtually ignored. Thus, Canadian authorities had considerable freedom to release Esquimalt garrison troops for overseas service, and some were actually released in time to be included in the first contingent of the expeditionary force. Until that point, however, Esquimalt had played the role envisaged for it, as a base of operations for the Royal Navy on the west coast of the Americas, giving Britain a position of strength and the capability of projecting its power southwards to the United States and the Pacific coastal nations of Central and South America.

In contrast, Halifax became the main embarkation port for troops proceeding overseas, and shipped an ever-growing share of food and war materiel destined for Britain. By 1917 German U-boats were operating in the western Atlantic, and a large fleet of minor war vessels was employed in escort and surveillance duties. Far from diminishing, the strategic importance of the base continued to grow, and the British continued to exert pressure to maintain the fortress at maximum strength, of course to the disadvantage of those of the garrison seeking active service.

In April 1915, before a large crowd in front of Province House, the people of Nova Scotia presented the 25th Battalion with two field kitchens and a cheque for $2,500 to purchase amenities. On May 20 another sad but enthusiastic crowd watched them sail for France in the liner *Saxonia*, which also carried Quebec's 22nd Battalion; the two would fight together throughout the war.

In 1915 a Royal Commission under the distinguished judge Sir Charles Davidson was established to inquire into rumours of misconduct in the purchase of war materials by the federal government. The most serious matter related to the acquisition of submarines by Sir Richard McBride, which was alleged to be questionable in six different respects.

The cheques in payment for the submarines were dated August 1, 1914, but the transaction was not completed until the 4th. It was determined that it was the practice of the provincial Finance Ministry that all cheques written between the 1st and 15th were dated the first day of the month. The Auditor-General testified that he actually signed the cheque at about 5 p.m. on August 4.

The actual purchase amount was $1,150,000, and this was the total of the cheques given to Paterson. But a clerical error decoding telegrams in Ottawa resulted in the figure of $1,050,000 being mentioned in the federal documentation. It was suspected that the $100,000 difference might have been misappropriated. In addition, there was no documented transfer of title to the federal government. The commission made it clear that the actual amount was $1,150,000, and that "Indubitable title lies in His Majesty, in the right of Canada."

Questions had been raised with respect to the fees paid to Captain Logan on his second mission to obtain torpedoes for the submarines. The British Columbia government had requested Ottawa to put a sum of $10,000 at his disposal, but this was never done. The mission was unsuccessful, and Logan presented a bill for services and expenses totalling $690, which was duly paid by the naval authorities. The commission confirmed that the amount was reasonable.

The commission heard much testimony on the fourth issue, the necessity for and the incidents arising in the course of the purchase. The commission confirmed the inadequacy of west-coast defences in relation to the international situation, and the sequence of events as described in Chapter Six. Admiral Kingsmill testified that "The fact of those submarines being there, I am perfectly certain in my own mind, saved the city of Victoria if not the city of Vancouver from serious damage." Admiral Storey fully supported that view. The commission concluded, "It can be asserted and without reserve, that the securement of the two submarines was highly desirable — indeed a very pressing necessity."

The fifth concern revolved around the efficiency of the submarines from a technical standpoint. In the first place it was known that the Chileans had serious doubts about the surfacing buoyance of the boats when fully loaded, hence their reluctance to complete the purchase. It was also believed that the boats required more ongoing maintenance and repairs than they should have done. As senior officer of submarines Lieutenant-Commander Keyes did indicate that *CC2* may have struck bottom while on trials for the Chileans, damaging a valve that was subsequently repaired. As evidence of their efficiency he pointed out that one or the other had been continuously on patrol since the purchase, and his opinion as to their efficiency was backed up by the dockyard's maintenance experts. The commission ruled that the two submarines were effective fighting machines.

(This opinion was subsequently confirmed by events. After three years of west-coast service *CC1* and *CC2* together with their depot ship *Shearwater* made the journey from Esquimalt to Halifax via the Panama Canal. As coastal submarines they were not designed for the open ocean, but the passage was made, albeit with considerable difficulty and severe hardship for the crews.)

The last issue concerned the price paid for the boats, which some considered excessive. The commission was obliged to consider allegations that it had been inflated to cover commissions to Captain Logan and the premier, the latter to the tune of half a million dollars. Sir Richard vehemently denied that he had been offered or received a penny, and no evidence was offered in support of the allegation, although a Victoria group had hired a detective agency to investigate. Captain Logan's testimony was bitter.

> *I never got any commission. The only thing*
> *I got was a lot of abuse since that time. I have*
> *heard nothing but dishonorable insinuations and*
> *innuendo for the last twelve months, and I have*
> *in a small way shared in the heap of abuse piled*
> *on the premier of this province. I feel indignant*
> *and disgusted over the whole thing; I think it*
> *is enough to make a man who is inclined to do*
> *anything for his country stand aside.*

It was thanks to political partisanship that the swirling rumours gained sufficient traction for the government to set up the Royal Commission. McBride and indeed Logan must have been gratified by its final statement.

> *It is cause for congratulation to all*
> *Canadians that this much discussed and*
> *criticised enterprise was, throughout, of*
> *blameless character. The acquisition of these*
> *submarines probably saved, as is believed by*
> *many, including high naval authorities, the cities*
> *of Victoria and Vancouver, or one or other of*
> *them, from attack and enormous tribute.*

Icing was one of the many problems confronting the ships on the New York patrol in winter.

> *What Sir Richard did in those days of anxiety,*
> *even distress, and what he accomplished deserves*
> *the commendation of his fellow countrymen.*
> *For his motives were those of patriotism, and his*
> *conduct that of an honourable man.*

Welcome as these words must have been, Richard McBride had had enough. For over a year he had been not only the premier of British Columbia but its de facto Minister of Defence, for much of the time the target of partisan innuendo and abuse. On December 15, 1915, he resigned, and became the province's Agent General in London. He died there in 1917, six days before his one-time British Columbia navy reached Halifax.

***

In rotation with the other ships of the 4th Cruiser Squadron, *Niobe* continued her demanding but monotonous New York patrols into the early months of 1915. The German liner *Prinz Eitel Friedrich* had been in the Far East at the outbreak of war. At Tsingtao she was converted to an armed merchant cruiser and placed under Admiral von Spee's command. On August 13 she was detached to act independently to interrupt trade in the South Pacific and South Atlantic, and became one of the most successful of the German raiders. Her whereabouts unknown to the allies, she entered the North Atlantic with the vague objective of finding her way back to Germany. On March 10, 1915, she unexpectedly arrived in Newport News, Virginia.

The first British reaction was to concentrate all the available cruisers off Newport News. Further analysis lead to the suspicion that *Prinz Eitel Friedrich*'s appearance was cover for a breakout by the German ships at New York; the cruisers were once again concentrated there, leaving *Niobe* alone until His Majesty's Ship *Cumberland* arrived in support. Either one had the speed and guns to destroy the raider if it emerged. Tension rose when the German ship was reported to have embarked a pilot preparatory to sailing, but the suspense ended on April 8 when she interned herself in the United States. When the Americans entered the war in 1917 she was commissioned as the United States Ship *Dekalb* and employed as a troopship.

By summer *Niobe*'s funnels were in serious condition, her boilers worn out and her bulkeads in bad shape. After returning from her final patrol on July 17, 1915, she never sailed again, finishing her career as a depot ship alongside a Halifax jetty.

The blockade in which she had played a minor part continued throughout the war, virtually cutting Germany off from the overseas world. In 1917 the Germans initiated unrestricted submarine warfare, which at one point seemed well on its way to bringing Britain to its knees. For some in authority, the war had become a question of which side could first succeed in starving out its opponent. With the introduction of the convoy system the allies blunted the U-boat threat, and the blockade proved unbreakable. Several hundred thousand more Germans are estimated to have perished between 1914 and 1919 than would have died if mortality rates had remained at prewar levels. Historians differ on the importance of the blockade in eroding the German will to fight, but all agree that it was significant. Central to the Royal Navy's ability to mount and sustain the blockade was its access to Halifax as a base of operations. And, until the United States decided to enter the war on the side of Britain and the Empire, the blockade stood as a constant reproach and reminder of Britain's military prowess to the Americans who favoured United States support for Germany in the war.

Halifax had welcomed the Blue Riband liner *Mauretania* in August 1914, when she took refuge in the port at the outbreak of war. She would be back, but in very different guise. After returning to the United Kingdom she spent a very short time as an armed merchant cruiser before it was realized that she was unsuited for that role due to her enormous coal consumption. She then became a troopship, carrying three thousand soldiers at a time to the Gallipoli battlefields; on one voyage she dodged a submarine torpedo by a violent course alteration reminiscent of her turn to Halifax in 1914. She underwent a further transformation to become a hospital ship carrying the wounded of Gallipoli to hospitals in Egypt. In camouflage paint her final wartime role was to carry Canadian troops to Europe from Halifax, after that port became the main embarkation point for men of the Canadian Expeditionary Force.

On December 6, 1917, Halifax harbour was the scene of the largest man-made explosion before the atomic bomb. The Norwegian ship *Imo* was leaving Bedford Basin as the French freighter *Mont Blanc* entered harbour. Although both carried

Halifax dockyard after the 1917 explosion. HMCS Niobe *suffered many casualties and serious damage..*

pilots they collided. The *Mont Blanc* carried a highly dangerous cargo of TNT, picric acid, benzol, and guncotton, but this information was not widely shared. A fire ignited by the collision quickly spread and the crew abandoned ship, which drifted and grounded on the Halifax side of the harbour, enveloped in flames.

Niobe dispatched her steam pinnace with a voluntary crew of seven. The tug *Stella Maris* was trying to tow *Mont Blanc* away from the shore, but the hawser snapped. At 9:04 a.m. there was a shattering explosion; when the smoke partially cleared *Mont Blanc* had completely disappeared, as had *Niobe*'s pinnace. Seven hundred yards away, *Niobe* herself was nearly torn from her moorings and suffered a great deal of superficial damage. Twenty members of her ship's company were killed, along with 1,600 civilians in the north end of the city, which was levelled.

After the explosion Lieutenant-Colonel R.B. Simmonds of the Princess Louise Fusiliers was put in charge of the army and navy relief parties. They found food and shelter for the families of overseas men and members of the garrison, and expedited repairs to more than 160 houses, earning the commendations from the minister of militia and the Halifax Relief Commission.

Midshipman William Maitland-Dougall volunteered for submarine service with the Royal Navy. He left *CC1* in late 1914 and travelled to the United Kingdom in one of the *H*-class submarines built for the British at the Canadian Vickers shipyard in Montreal. Thereafter he served with distinction in British submarines patrolling the North Sea, rising to lieutenant and command of submarine *D3*. On March 12, 1917, his boat was operating surfaced in the English Channel. Although German submarines were active, they had no ships or aircraft in the Channel. Events had shown that the biggest risk for a surfaced British submarine was that it would be mistaken for an enemy and attacked by friendly forces. Standing orders were that they should remain on the surface and exchange identities with the ship or aircraft, presumed to be friendly unless proved otherwise. Diving to escape was the last resort. Operational cooperation between France and Britain in the Channel was poor, although liaison officers from the other navy were present in the headquarters at Dover and Calais.

On a partly cloudy but clear day *E3* was spotted by a French airship. Assuming the submarine to be German the airship approached out of the sun for an attack. Maitland-Dougall discharged recognition flares, but the French had no information about such signals and thought they were being fired at. Their first bombing run failed, and in disregard of standing orders *E3* began to dive to escape. But the boat was still partly visible when a second bomb was released and scored a hit. Some men were seen in the water, and called to the airship in English, but none of the crew survived despite intensive rescue efforts.

The death of Maitland-Dougall and those of his classmates at Coronel meant that five of the twenty graduates of the first class at the Royal Naval College of Canada were killed in the First

World War. There has been speculation that the leadership of the navy in the Second World War might have been much different had this group survived.

Arthur Currie, former commanding officer of the 5th Regiment of militia garrison artillery, led a brigade in the 1st Division of the expeditionary force. He distinguished himself in the Canadian's first battle at Ypres in 1915 and earned successive promotions until he rose to command the Canadian Corps of four divisions, with the rank of lieutenant-general. He was knighted and after the war became chancellor of McGill University. At some point and after some controversy his old debt to his former regiment was discharged.

On only one occasion in the First World War did a Canadian fortress fire a shot in anger, mistakenly, but consistent with orders. The firing arcs of many guns in the Halifax defences covered wide and deep tracts of land on both sides of the harbour, and if badly directed their shells could land from the shoreline to well inland. The risk had long been recognized, but under strict control the batteries frequently practiced against towed targets using dummy ammunition.

However, in time of war defence of the fortress took precedence. The examination gun at Fort McNab was under strict instructions to prevent uncleared vessels from proceeding up-harbour, first with warning shots, but if necessary by direct fire without waiting for further orders. Inevitably the shots would be in the direction of the city.

On March 1, 1915, shortly after noon, a twenty-five-year-old woman named Alice O'Brien returned from a ride to her family's house at number 10 Lucknow Street in south-end Halifax. She found the neighbourhood in an uproar. An explosion had just occurred on the roof of the partition separating her home from the next door neighbour's at number 12. Windows were shattered and scraps of wood littered the pavement. At the time the only occupants of the houses had been the two maids, both of whom had very fortunately been hanging out the washing in the backyards.

At first it was suspected that a gas explosion had occurred. But soon unmistakable evidence was found to show that the houses had been struck by a shell of British manufacture. In fact, a projectile fired from Fort McNab battery had ricocheted off the water and travelled 3,700 yards inland to wreak destruction in the quiet neighbourhood.

The incident had begun several hours earlier when the Marine and Fisheries vessel *Brant* had left the inner harbour on one of her routine buoy-tending tasks, on this occasion off McNabs Island. Her route took her into the examination anchorage established by the navy at the beginning of the war. As long as she did not go farther out than the examination vessel at the southern boundary of the anchorage the navy did not require her to obtain clearance before returning to harbour. Her task completed, at about 11:45 she started to return to her berth at slow speed, always having remained to the north of the examination vessel. Her captain was having lunch below when he heard a shot that he assumed was the noon gun from the citadel, but on hearing a second shot he came on deck.

The rounds had come from the always alert and loaded examination gun at Fort McNab, under strict orders to fire warning shots at vessels leaving the anchorage without clearance. Since the appropriate flag signal was not being flown the examination gun's crew knew that *Brant* had not obtained clearance, but did not know that there was no need for her to do so.

Security demanded that the examination gun required freedom to fire warnings with live rounds, even though shots from Fort McNab would inevitably be aimed toward the city. Under the Defence Scheme, the role had initially been assigned to a six-inch weapon in the fort. But during target practice a hundred-pound inert projectile had rebounded from the surface and had landed in a farmer's field six miles inland. Alerted to the danger, the authorities replaced the 6-inch examination gun with a 6-pounder. Had the original still been in use a disaster might well have ensued.

Ironically, to prevent the sort of accident that had just occurred, the Defence Scheme had obligated vessels employed within the harbour to permanently display identification exempting them from clearance. Under the pressure of events at the outbreak of war the overstretched navy had failed to implement the provision.

In 1914 there were approximately sixty fortresses or defended ports in the British Empire. In the four years of war that followed only two came into action.

The German light cruiser *Emden* had been detached from von Spee's squadron before the war began, and embarked on a spectacular career of trade disruption and shore bombardment as soon as hostilities commenced. One of Captain Karl von Müller's exploits was to enter the undefended port of Penang in Malaya and sink the unsuspecting Russian cruiser *Zhemchug* and a French destroyer. On September 22, 1914, she bombarded the Indian port of Madras, setting fire to the oil tanks on the sea front. At this point she was engaged by two 4.7-inch quick-firing guns of the Madras Volunteer Artillery, actually field guns, but emplaced for coast defence. Without a base, Captain Müller knew that he could not afford to sustain damage and was forced to withdraw and continue his depredations elsewhere. Tracked down by the Australian cruiser *Sydney*, the raider was finally destroyed while attacking the wireless station at Direction Island in the Cocos on November 7, 1914.

The second incident was a more serious affair. On the morning of November 3, 1914, three German battle cruisers had sortied across the North Sea to bombard the English town of

Yarmouth with their 11-inch guns. In poor visibility their shells fell harmlessly on the beaches or into the sea, but they were able to return safely despite being pursued by British forces.

A second raid was planned. This time the intended targets were the coastal towns of Scarborough and Hartlepool. The force was to consist of the battle cruisers *Seydlitz, Moltke, Von der Tann*, and *Derfflinger*, and the heavy cruiser *Blücher*, with the whole High Seas Fleet standing by to cover their escape. *Von der Tann* and *Derfflinger* proceeded to bombard Scarborough, an undefended holiday destination with no military installations. From close range they inflicted civilian casualties and considerable property damage before withdrawing.

The other three ships were destined for Hartlepool, in which two British destroyers and a submarine were anchored. The coastal defences consisted of Heugh battery, with two 6-inch guns, and Lighthouse battery, with one, all identical to the 6-inch guns in the Canadian fortresses. The two batteries were relatively close together, and in rear of Heugh battery was the fire command post. They were manned by eleven officers and 155 other ranks, including a few regulars, but the vast majority were men of the Territorial Army; "militia," in the Canadian context. As was usual at dawn all were at their stations.

At 8:10 a.m. the leading German ship opened fire, and for fifteen minutes *Moltke, Von der Tann*, and *Blücher* all concentrated on the batteries, from ranges of between four and five thousand yards. The Heugh battery engaged the battle cruisers, and the Lighthouse battery the *Blücher*. Hits were obtained on *Moltke* and *Blücher*, which had some of its secondary armament put out of action. An early German shot knocked out communications between the fire command post and the batteries, which thereafter acted independently in accordance with well-practised emergency drills.

In accordance with their plan the two battle cruisers then

bombarded the harbour installations for thirty minutes with their 11-inch guns, while *Blücher*'s 8.2-inch weapons continued to engage the batteries, both of which could now concentrate on her. The three British warships attempted to sortie, but one of the destroyers was damaged and driven ashore, and the other could not clear the bar. The submarine was forced to dive in the shallow water, struck the bottom, and took no part in the action.

As the battle cruisers withdrew they again shelled the batteries, which continued to engage them out to 9,200 yards, all three guns having been in action for forty-two minutes, and having fired 123 rounds. The defending gunners suffered only two casualties, both killed. Again the raiding force returned to home port without losing a ship.

Admittedly, the heavily armoured German ships succeeded in accomplishing their mission. But the result confirmed that well-manned forts could still survive an engagement against opponents having a great superiority of numbers and calibres of guns. Probably in case they were intercepted by British naval forces, the Germans were using armour-piercing shells with delayed-action fuses. These shells were not designed for shore bombardment, and often rebounded, not exploding until they landed in the town behind the batteries. Also, the flat trajectory of naval weapons at short ranges meant that a direct hit had to be obtained in order to knock out a coastal gun. In the ill-fated attack on the Dardanelles, the Royal Navy would soon relearn the old lesson that ships could not defeat forts.

***

Had the Halifax or Esquimalt defences been challenged by the German light cruisers actually present on the two coasts the situation would have been very different in two ways. In that scenario the attackers would have faced weapons of a larger calibre than their own, and without armour protection could not have survived the same punishment as the Hartlepool raiders. In practice, given their lack of a repair base they could not have tolerated any significant damage whatsoever. Had the enemy ever seriously considered an attack on one of the fortresses it may be assumed that the idea was quickly abandoned. However, the same considerations would not have deterred a raid on an undefended port to obtain coal or to terrorize the population.

Mr. Harry Piers concluded his monumental study of the Halifax fortress with the following words.

> *Since 1749 Halifax has never been invested or even attacked. While the city may not have the glorious associations, romantic atmosphere, and stirring traditions, so abundantly connected with venerable places like Louisbourg or Annapolis Royal, we can only be most heartily thankful for our safety. We must never forget, however, that our nearly two centuries of peace has been due in large measure to our military strength.*

The same sentiments would apply equally to her sister fortress at Victoria.

ACKNOWLEDGEMENTS

More people than I can properly acknowledge have helped make this book possible. Primary records of this little-known aspect of the vast history of the Great War are very scarce, but everywhere I received enthusiastic help in bringing them to light.

An all too brief research visit to Victoria was successful thanks to many helpers. At the Canadian Forces Base (CFB) Esquimalt Naval and Military Museum Joseph Lenarcik guided me through the records and pointed me to other sources. The archives of the Municipality of Esquimalt were surprisingly rich and well-catalogued, and the staff led by the very knowledgeable Gregory Evans gave me every possible assistance. At the Maritime Museum of British Columbia my friend and former naval colleague Jan Drent went out of his way to make my visit a very rewarding one. Another old friend, Larry Dawe, introduced me to individuals whose help yielded information I would never have found on my own.

The regimental museum of 5th Field Regiment Royal Canadian Artillery at Victoria's Bay Street militia armouries is one of the best of its kind that I have visited. Very importantly for my purposes, its archival records are extensive and easily retrievable and the staff most knowledgeable and helpful. My special thanks go to museum volunteers Craig Cotter and Dale Murray for their informed and generous support at the time and subsequently.

Regrettably, the militia units at Halifax have not been able to preserve their histories to the same extent. However, thanks to the assistance of Major Gary Melville, Commanding Officer of the Halifax Rifles; Captain Murray Roesler, adjutant of the 1st Regiment Royal Canadian Artillery; and Second Lieutenant Andrew McNeil of the Princess Louise Fusiliers, I had full access to what was available and derived much useful information. The very efficient staff at Nova Scotia Archives and Records

Management were extremely helpful; I owe much to Gary Shutlak in particular. Mr. Royce Walker of the Friends of McNabs Island Society very generously helped me with essential details of that important fortified area, and Dan Conlin and Linda Silver gave me every assistance in accessing the research resources of the Maritime Museum of the Atlantic. As always Rick Sanderson at the Maritime Command Museum was a great support.

I would be very remiss if I failed to thank the staff at Formac Publishing for their usual professional assistance; Kathy Chapman and Nicole Habib were very helpful guides through the editing and production process.

It is impossible to adequately express my thanks to Dr. Roger Sarty, Professor of Naval and Military History at Wilfrid Laurier University. He was exceptionally forthcoming with advice and documentary assistance throughout the process. Of critical importance, he very generously allowed me access to his unpublished doctoral dissertation "Silent Sentry," containing, *inter alia*, an exhaustive academic treatment of the background and events in which I was interested. Without that framework the book could simply not have been written. I remain eternally in his debt.

Finally, I acknowledge my own entire responsibility for any shortcomings that may have survived.

APPENDIX
Coastal Defences

In the 1540s King Henry VIII began to build coastal fortifications armed and fortified to repel attacks by ships carrying the smooth-bore cannon that were beginning to come into common use. Their first guns were naval guns simply remounted on the fortress ramparts. Ever since, the various calibres of coastal artillery have tended to be the same as those used in the ships of the time, although their mountings would differ.

In peacetime the early coastal defences were manned by a small garrison, commanded by a master gunner, sufficient only to maintain the weapons and works, but also providing the trained and expert nucleus of the wartime complement. Their duties also included ". . . to teach such of the inhabitants as shall be inclinable to learn how to load, point and fire the guns placed there for their defence." In war, additional trained or untrained manpower needed to be drawn from various sources to work all the weapons. This pattern endured throughout the history of coastal artillery in the British Empire.

Since the earliest times guns have fired two types of payload, shot and shell. The former was made of solid iron, the weight of the projectile commonly being used to indicate the calibre of the gun, e.g., the 24-pounder, a standard ship's weapon for centuries. The shot could be round or cylindrical. Effective at close range against wooden ships and masonry forts, solid shot was virtually useless against armoured targets. By 1914 it was used for target practice only.

As its name implies, a shell consists of a hollow iron or steel body, either spherical or cylindrical, its central void filled with an explosive charge and fitted with a fuse to explode it at the end of its flight. At first, fuses had to be cut to a length corresponding with the desired range, to a large extent a matter of guesswork. They were lit manually on loading, or by the flame of the exploding propellant on firing. The advent of rifling for large weapons made them sufficiently accurate for the shell to be triggered on impact by a percussion fuse in the nose. Alternatively, clockwork fuses were employed to set a range at which the shell would explode over the target.

Until the middle of the nineteenth century the muzzle-loading smooth-bore cannon firing solid round shot or explosive shell continued in use, both ashore and afloat; but after the Crimean War the next seventy-five years saw rapid evolution.

It had long been known that a rotating projectile would achieve greater accuracy, but it was not until the mid-nineteenth century that technology made it possible. At first studs on the projectile engaged with twisting grooves inside the barrel, but this allowed some of the propelling gas to escape. The solution was to incorporate a driving band on the projectile, to act as a gas seal and at the same time to engage with the rifling to impart the desired spin.

Rifling of the bore to give the projectile a spin improved accuracy and destructive power, leading to universal introduction of the rifled muzzle-loader by the 1870s, and the concomitant redesign of coastal defences. Meanwhile, experimentation had continued with loading from the breech or rear of the gun rather than from the muzzle. By 1885 work began to replace muzzle-loaders with breech-loaders, again generating major remodelling of the forts and batteries.

In 1914 virtually all coastal weapons were breech-loaders. Because of the weight of their projectiles larger calibre guns required the projectiles to be loaded first, followed by a separate propelling charge. In smaller weapons the charge and projectile could be combined in a single package, thus greatly improving the rate of fire. A common standard was that for sustained fire projectile and charge packaged together should not exceed eighty pounds in weight. Such weapons were designated quick-firers. The same term was also used for guns where charge and projectile were loaded in sequence, as long as the charge was in a brass case rather than in silk bags.

The guns had been standardized in four types, Cordite being the propellant for all calibres:

- Long-range 9.2-inch Mk. X, range 17,400 yards, firing 380-pound common, armour-piercing, Lyddite or shrapnel shells.
- Medium-range 6-inch Mk. VII, mounted *en barbette*, range 12,600 yards, firing 100-pound shells of the same types as the 9.2-inch. Disappearing guns of the same calibre were still in use at Esquimalt at the outbreak of the First World War.
- Medium-range 4.7-inch quick-firer Mk. III, range 11,800 yards, firing 45-pound shells of the same types as above, except shrapnel.
- Short-range 12-pounder quick-firer, range 8,000 yards, firing 12-pound common or Lyddite shells at a rate of about fifteen rounds per minute per gun.

Common shell was so named because it could be used against a variety of targets. It was filled with gunpowder, which burst rather than detonated, and had some incendiary effect. Large fragments continued along the shell's trajectory.

By the First World War common shell was well on the way to being replaced with Lyddite, or common Lyddite as it became known. The shell was filled with solidified picric acid, a powerful explosive much more effective than gunpowder, and had some penetration power against steel armour. On detonating there was no incendiary effect, and the shell disintegrated into many small fragments dispersed in all directions.

As its name implies, armour-piercing shell was specially designed to penetrate a ship's protective shield before exploding. This capability was based on a more pointed shell design, a hardened nose cap, and a special delay fuse to withstand the shock of impact and allow the projectile to explode inside the armoured belt.

Shrapnel shell was named after its inventor, Colonel Henry Shrapnel of the British army. It was a cylindrical casing containing several hundred half-inch balls. The fuse was set to ignite the casing's gunpowder charge about 150 yards in front of and sixty feet above the target. The balls were then expelled at a velocity of 200–250 feet per second to be added to the 150–200 feet per second of the projectile, hitting the surface in a conical pattern 250 yards by 30 yards. This was an anti-personnel weapon only, suitable in the coastal defence scenario for countering enemy landings.

The extraordinary development of warships and guns presented the coastal gunner with unprecedented problems. His target would be moving much more quickly and often much further from the battery. It was necessary to find a means of continuously ascertaining the position of the target as it steamed through the water. In the 1880s Captain H.S. Watkin of the Royal

Artillery invented the depression range finder and the position finder. Both were based on the principle of the right-angled triangle and on the accurately known height of the instrument above sea level. When laid on the bow waterline of the target the instrument's angle of depression allowed the horizontal range to be calculated automatically. Both instruments recorded a target's range, and the position finder its bearing also.

Increasing use of electricity allowed the information to be transmitted directly to the guns by means of dials. The trainer sighted on the target and the correct elevation for the measured range was applied to the sights automatically. The position finder was used with the 9.2-inch guns, the depression range finder with the smaller calibres.

These arrangements worked well for targets at medium to long ranges, but could not deal with the torpedo boat, destroyer, or blockship making a high-speed entry at night. The first step in solving that problem was the development of defence electric lights. They emitted a narrow, focussed beam with which to search for, locate, and track a target. Alternatively, they could be used with dispersed beams to create an illuminated area through which the attacker would have to pass.

Fast close-in targets had to be hit as soon as detected. The solution was the automatic sight. When laid by the layer on the bow waterline of the target, the sight automatically applied the correct elevation to the gun. When the sight was properly adjusted the first rounds would be either on or very near the target.

There would be very little warning of a night attack by numerous and speedy torpedo boats and destroyers, and no time for ranging by spotting the fall of shot and correcting accordingly. A high-speed target would not remain very long in the illuminated area, and thus would be exposed to fire for only a very brief period. One minute was the expected duration; planning and training were based on that assumption. The gun crews were organized in watches, the duty watch being on alert and close to the loaded guns. A lookout peered continually into the illuminated area. A well-thought-out distribution of fire plan had to be understood and practised by everyone in the battery, to ensure that all targets were engaged and that the first shot was a hit.

An elaborate organization was required to maximize the defensive power of a coastal fortress. The navy had its own tasks and worked closely with the army, but was not under the command of the fortress commander. At each defended location that officer was responsible for coastal and landward defences, and for the garrison of artillery, engineers, infantry, and supporting arms. Garrison artillery was responsible for the tactical control of searchlights and the artillery armament, both the fixed seaward guns and the mobile field artillery for landward defence. Engineers maintained the fortifications and electrical communications and operated the searchlights, as well as providing normal engineering services. The infantry manned the entrenchments, protecting batteries and searchlights and guarding landing places and countering enemy forces that might succeed in getting ashore.

Below the fortress commander, fire commanders had the most important tactical role. Each commanded a group of batteries in the same area, known as a fire command. The batteries could be of different calibres depending on the geography of the fortress, but each battery consisted of guns of the same calibre, usually no more than four.

An engagement would begin by the detection of a target. Its range and bearing would be determined from the fire command post using its position finder. The position would then be plotted on a large-scale plan of the harbour approaches, overlaid with a grid pattern of squares, each with an alphanumeric designation. The fire commander would assign the target to the most suitable battery commander and pass its grid location. The battery would train on the location, use its own position or range finder to apply the correct range to the sights, along with throw-off or deflection settings based on the range and estimated course and speed of the target. It would then report "Ready to engage" and await the order to open fire. At night diffused-beam searchlights were directly under the control of the fire commanders, while focussed searchlights were allocated to battery commanders.

In Chapter Three mention was made of submarine mining, a component of the Empire's port defences, in place for a time at both Halifax and Esquimalt, but discontinued before the war. At different periods that duty was assigned to either the Royal Engineers or to the navy, and in the latter case to the Royal Marine Artillery.

The mines employed were of the moored variety. In the main channel they were laid at a depth such that the deepest-draft friendly ships using the port would pass safely above them. These main-channel mines were not in fact set to explode on contact. Instead, personnel in an observation station ashore would electrically trigger a particular mine when an attacker passed above it.

The main channel would be well-buoyed in time of war, and the areas outside that channel would be forbidden to allied traffic. In the forbidden area active contact mines would be set to an appropriate depth to destroy an enemy ship or submarine unfortunate enough to stray out of the deep channel.

BIBLIOGRAPHY

Berger, Carl, ed. *Imperialism and Nationalism 1884–1914.* Toronto: Copp Clark, 1969.

Campbell, Duncan A. *Unlikely Allies.* London: Hambledon Continuum, 2007.

Careless, J.M.S. "Submarines, Princes and Hollywood Commandos." In *British Columbia; Patterns in Economic, Political and Cultural Development,* edited by Dickson M. Falconer. Victoria, B.C.: Camosun College, 1982.

Cuthbertson, Brian. *Halifax and its People.* Halifax: Nimbus, 1999.

———. *The Halifax Citadel.* Halifax: Formac, 2001.

Cook, Tim. *The Madman and the Butcher.* Toronto: Penguin Canada, 2010.

Davidson, Sir Charles. *Report of the Royal Commission on the Purchase of Submarines.* Ottawa: King's Printer, 1917.

Duguid, A.F. *From the Outbreak of War to the Formation of the Canadian Corps, August 1914–September 1915.* Vol. 1 of *Official History of the Canadian Forces in the Great War 1914–1918.* Ottawa: King's Printer, 1938.

Elson, Bryan. *First to Die.* Halifax: Formac, 2010.

Ferguson, Julie H. *Through a Canadian Periscope.* Toronto: Dundurn Press, 1995.

Gimblett, Richard H., ed. *The Naval Service of Canada, 1910–2010.* Toronto: Dundurn Press, 2009.

Granatstein, Jack. *Canada's Army,* 2nd ed. Toronto: University of Toronto Publishing, 2011.

———, and Dean F. Oliver. *The Oxford Companion to Canadian Military History.* Toronto: Oxford University Press, 2011.

Gregson, Harry. *A History of Victoria 1842–1970.* Vancouver: J.J. Douglas, 1970.

Gurney-Smith, Marilyn. *The King's Yard.* Halifax: Nimbus Publishing, 1985.

Gwyn, Julian. *Ashore and Afloat.* Ottawa: University of Ottawa Press, 2004.

Hadley, Michael, Rob Huebert and Fred W. Crickard, eds. *A Nation's Navy.* Montreal and Kingston: McGill-Queen's University Press, 1996.

Hadley, Michael, and Roger Sarty. *Tin Pots and Pirate Ships.* Kingston: McGill-Queen's University Press, 1988.

Hunt, M.S. *Nova Scotia's Part in the Great War.* Halifax: Veterans Publishing Company, 1920.

Johnston, A.I.B. *Defending Halifax: Ordnance, 1825–1906.* Ottawa: Parks Canada, 1981.

Johnston, William, G.P. Rawling, Richard H. Gimblett, and John MacFarlane. *The Seabound Coast.* Toronto: Dundurn Press, 2010.

Kitchen, Martin. "The German Invasion of Canada in the First World War." *International History Review* 7, no. 2 (May, 1985).

Lovatt, Ronald. *Shoot, Shoot, Shoot.* Victoria, B.C.: Rodd Hill Friends Society, 1993.

Maurice-Jones, Col. K.W. *The History of Coast Artillery in the British Army.* Uckfield, Sussex: The Naval and Military Press Ltd., no date.

McKee, Fraser. *The Armed Yachts of Canada.* Erin, Ontario: Boston Mills Press, 1983.

McNaught, Siobhan J. "The Rise of Proto-nationalism: Sir Wilfrid Laurier and the Founding of the Naval Service of Canada." In *A Nation's Navy,* edited by Michael L. Hadley, Rob Huebert and Fred W. Crickard. Montreal and Kingston: McGill-Queen's University Press, 1996.

Milner, Marc. *Canada's Navy, The First Century.* Toronto: University of Toronto Press, 1999.

Nova Scotia Archives and Records Management. *Halifax and its People.* Halifax: Nimbus Publishing, 1999.

O'Regan, May C. "Raider's Threat Speeds Liner to Port of Safety," *Port and Province,* March, 1933.

Ormsby, Margaret A. *British Columbia, A History.* Vancouver: Macmillan of Canada, 1958.

Parker, Mike. *Fortress Halifax.* Halifax: Nimbus, 2004.

Perkins, Dave. *Canada's Submariners, 1914–1923.* Erin, Ontario: Boston Mills Press, 1989.

Piers, Harry, G.M. Self and Phyllis Ruth Blakeley. *The Evolution of Halifax Fortress 1749–1928.* Halifax: Public Archives of Nova Scotia, 1947.

Penlington, Norman. *The Alaska Boundary Dispute, A Critical Appraisal.* Toronto: McGraw-Hill Ryerson, 1972.

———. *Canada and Imperialism 1896–1899.* Toronto: University of Toronto Press, 1965.

Preston, Andrew. *Sword of the Spirit, Shield of Faith.* New York: Alfred A. Knopf, 2012.

Raddall, Thomas H. *Halifax, Warden of the North.* Halifax: Nimbus, 2010.

Robertson, Lt. Col. F.A. "Early History of 5 (British Columbia) Field Regiment, Royal Regiment of Canadian Artillery." Unpublished manuscript, 1925.

Sarty, Roger. *Halifax and the Defence of Canada 1906–1919.* Papers of the Canadian Historical Association, 1981.

———. "Incident on Lucknow Street, Defenders and Defended in Halifax, 1915." *Canadian Military History* 10, no. 2 (Article 5, 2001).

———. "Silent Sentry: A Military and Political History of Canadian Coast Defence, 1860–1945." Ph.D. Dissertation University of Toronto, 1982.

———, and Barry Gough. "Sailors and Soldiers: The Royal Navy, the Canadian Forces, and the Defence of Atlantic Canada. In *A Nation's Navy,* edited by Michael L. Hadley, Rob Huebert and Fred W. Crickard. Montreal: McGill-Queen's University Press, 1996.

Tennyson, Brian, and Roger Sarty. *Sydney, Cape Breton and the Atlantic Wars.* Toronto: University of Toronto Press, 1999.

Tucker, G.N. *The Naval Service of Canada,* Vol. I. Ottawa: King's Printer, 1952.

Tweedie, Graham R. "The Roots of the Royal Canadian Navy, Sovereignty Versus Nationalism, 1812–1910." In *A Nation's Navy,* edited by Michael Hadley, Rob Huebert and Fred W. Crickard. Montreal and Kingston: McGill-Queen's University Press, 1996.

PHOTO CREDITS

5th Regiment Archives: p. 55, 204

Canada's Navy Centre: p. 198

Canadian War Museum: p. 91 (19890167-005), 96 (19790602-053), 203 (19890167-003), 211 (20030174-045)

Cuthbertson, Brian. *Halifax and its People.* Halifax: Nimbus, 1999: p. 60

———. *The Halifax Citadel: Portrait of a Military Fortress.* Halifax: Formac Publishing Company, 2011: front cover; p. 14, 15

British Columbia Provincial Archives: p. 25 (B-00245)

Department of National Defence Archives: front cover (C191, E-60722)); back cover (E-60722); p. 88 (0-220), 200 (SMSLEIPZIG-03), 231 (C191), 237 (E-38800)

Elson, Bryan: p. 115, 118

Elson, Bryan. *First to Die.* Halifax: Formac Publishing Company, 2010: front cover; back cover; p. 50, 72, 98, 125, 172, 210, 232, 234, 236

Johnston, William, G.P. Rawling, Richard H. Gimblett, and John MacFarlane. *The Seabound Coast.* Toronto: Dundurn Press, 2010: p. 116, 120, 190

Library and Archives Canada: p. 107 (PA 034016), 124 (PA 012223), 167 (PA 115374), 168 (PA 066841)

Maritime Command Museum, Halifax: p. 150 (HMCTB Tuna), 171, 193

Maritime Museum of the Atlantic: p. 157

Maritime Museum of British Columbia: p. 174

Milner, Marc. *Canada's Navy, The First Century.* Toronto: University of Toronto Press, 1999: p. 246

Nova Scotia Archives and Records Management: front cover; p. 28 (625530), 47, 59 (Army ACC 695), 71 (Army ACC 9241), 135, 226 (201404089)

———. Notman Collection: p. 39, 48 (12324), 54 (9999), 81 (68091), 86 (8884), 97, 101, 113 (54), 119 (6981), 145 (8108), 152 (15425)

———. Royal Engineers: p. 41 (#93 ACC 6990), 46 (#262 ACC 6892), 51 (#225 ACC 6995), 52 (#225 ACC 6905)

Ormsby, Margaret A. *British Columbia: A History.* Vancouver: Macmillan of Canada, 1958: p. 105, 108

Parker, Mike. *Fortress Halifax.* Halifax: Nimbus, 2004: back cover; p. 53, 58, 112, 131, 132, 134, 136

Perkins, Dave. *Canada's Submariners, 1914–1923.* Erin, Ontario: Boston Mills Press, 1989: p. 196

Piers, Harry, G.M. Self and Phyllis Ruth Blakeley. *The Evolution of Halifax Fortress 1749–1928.* Halifax: Public Archives of Nova Scotia, 1947: p. 75

Sarty, Roger. "Silent Sentry: A Military and Political History of Canadian Coast Defence, 1860–1945." Ph.D. Dissertation University of Toronto, 1982: p. 138, 164

Royal BC Museum, BC Archives, courtesy of: p. 182 (01410)

Tucker, G.N. *The Naval Service of Canada,* Vol. 1. Ottawa: King's Printer, 1952: front cover; back cover; p. 57, 64, 89, 93, 110, 178, 181, 216, 249

Tweedie, Graham R. "The Roots of the Royal Canadian Navy, Sovereignty Versus Nationalism, 1812–1910." In *A Nation's Navy,* edited by Michael Hadley, Rob Huebert and Fred W. Crickard. Montreal and Kingston: McGill-Queen's University Press, 1996: p. 240

INDEX